WITHDRAWN

The
Gospel
from
Outer
Space

Also by Robert Short

THE GOSPEL ACCORDING TO PEANUTS ®
"A fascinating book. . . . Robert L. Short is one of the most urbane
and erudite interpreters of Christianity going." —*Dighby Diehl*

THE PARABLES OF PEANUTS ®
"This new book is filled with wonderful quotes and is a real delight
from beginning to end. Actually, I could not possibly be more
pleased." —*Charles Schulz,* creator of *Peanuts* ®

SOMETHING TO BELIEVE IN
"Robert Short has thrown a major challenge to all churches. . . .
Something to Believe In is something to be considered seriously—in
spite of all the welcome hilarity of the illustrative material."
—*Toronto Star*

A TIME TO BE BORN—A TIME TO DIE
"An enterprising and ingenious project . . . cogently thought out, with
many relevant and illuminating quotations from a wide variety of
other writers." —*Malcolm Muggeridge*

The Gospel from Outer Space

Robert Short

1817

HARPER & ROW, PUBLISHERS, San Francisco

Cambridge, Hagerstown, New York, Philadelphia

London, Mexico City, São Paulo, Sydney

"Hitler posing before the bust of Hitler" (page 22), G.D.K.L., Weimar, is from H. F. Peters's *Zarathustra's Sister* (New York: Crown, 1977).

All Scripture quotations not otherwise identified are from the Revised Standard Version of the Bible, copyrighted 1946, 1952, © 1971, 1973.

FIRST EDITION

Designed by Design Office Bruce Kortebein

Library of Congress Cataloging in Publication Data

Short, Robert L.
THE GOSPEL FROM OUTER SPACE.

Includes bibliographical references.
1. Christianity—20th century. 2. Space theology. 3. Fantastic films—History and criticism. 4. Science fiction films—History and criticism.
I. Title.
BR481.S53   1982   230   82–18751
ISBN 0-06-067376-1 (pbk.)

83 84 85 86 87 10 9 8 7 6 5 4 3 2 1

To my son, Christopher Daniel Short

—age six. As Elliott says of his new friend, E.T., so I of Chris: "I love him. . . . He's the best little guy I ever met."
  As a "Christ-opher," Chris is a "Christ-bearer" whether he knows it or not, just as we all are. I hope and pray that he soon comes to know it. It would be wonderful if we'd all come to know it sooner, rather than later.

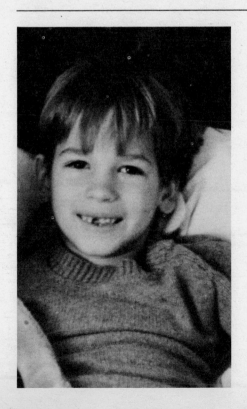

Contents

Foreword

This book is based on "The Religion of Outer Space," a color slide program I've been presenting for about the last three years. In form and content it very closely follows that program—a program in which, in addition to my own commentary, I use slides of cartoons, slides of movie stills, and slides of quotations. I'm grateful that this program has been a popular one, and I've always enjoyed doing it and getting the helpful feedback I've received from university, church, and high school audiences.

But up until just recently I've always felt that something was still missing from this program. I knew there were still many other important things I wanted to say, but I hadn't yet found *the* film I was looking for to help me say them and bring the presentation to the conclusion I wanted to build it up to.

That was before I saw *E.T.* Seeing *E.T.* for the first time was not only a pure delight, it was also a shock of recognition. I felt as if I'd finally found the solid cornerstone I'd been seeking for "The Religion of Outer Space."

But it wasn't until some days later that Clayton Carlson, my friend and editor at Harper & Row San Francisco, called up and announced that it was now time for me to write *The Gospel from Outer Space.* And just as Clayton had been delighted and excited by the film *E.T.,* I was delighted and excited by his suggestion—only slightly embarrassed that I hadn't thought of the idea first and called him. Anyway, Clayt, thanks. You do what a good editor should do: bring focus and direction into a scatterbrained author's head.

Thanks also to Ethelyn Bond, my good friend who for many years now has always done a first-class job of typing my manuscripts and deciphering the illegible. Friend Alicia Crawford was invaluable in the "*E.T.* Research" department.

And thanks to lovely Kay, my wife—

For thy sweet love remembered such wealth brings
That then I scorn to change my state with kings.

Religion and Outer Space

Today's Search for Meaning

Not so long ago in the history of the Western world, most people felt they had "someone to look up to"—namely, Christ, who gave their lives hope, direction, meaning, order, purpose, satisfaction, and fulfillment. Although these people knew they had scant *knowledge* of a lot of things in the world about them, they still felt they had scads of *understanding* of what life and the world were all about. They believed they had, through Jesus Christ, a good understanding of everything that was going on.

Nowadays, however, the situation is just the opposite—that is, we have a lot of clear, certain *knowledge* of almost everything about everything, but there's little *understanding* of what it's all about. This is why we all tend to be so nervous nowadays:

1

The Gospel from Outer Space

So the situation today is

> *Lots of knowledge, but little understanding*
> *Lots of means, but little meaning*
> *Lots of know-how, but little know-why*
> *Lots of sight, but little insight*

This situation is a constant drain on the very center of our lives. For nothing is more demeaning to the human spirit than meaninglessness. Nothing is harder for us to stand than the lack of ultimate understanding.

THE SMALL SOCIETY

Washington Star Syndicate, Inc.

HOO-BOY! IT'S A TERRIBLE THING TO KNOW WHAT'S GOING ON IN THE WORLD...

AND NOT UNDERSTAND IT—

Washington Star Syndicate, Inc.

10-10   BRICKMAN

To an enormous extent, "Christendom" has turned away from Christ, and no doubt it is for this very reason that there is such a lack of understanding and meaning today in the so-called Christian world. The Bible has always been very clear about this essential interrelation between God and understanding. Saint Paul, for instance, is quoting the Old Testament when he says: "No one understands, no one seeks for God" (Rom. 3:11, cf. Ps. 14:2). Strange to say, however, it was largely Christendom's own understanding of Christ that produced this wholesale defection from Christ in the first place. And this happened in two ways:

First, because we began to *mis*understand Christianity as a faith based primarily on *fear,* we became readier and readier to get rid of this harsh, vindictive God and to replace him—just as soon as possible—with some other god. At certain times in history this adolescent God given to moral temper tantrums may have supplied people with a certain amount of low-grade meaning for their lives.

Religion and Outer Space

But insofar as people were still deathly afraid of God, they usually were super-glad to see *this* God pushed out of the picture at the very first opportunity.

Secondly, it was largely Christianity itself that paved the way for all of this Western knowledge and means and know-how and reliance on what can be seen. For many Christians correctly understood that if God *alone* was the supernatural, then nature couldn't contain anything supernatural to harm us. If only God was God, then nature was only nature. Nature was no longer haunted by spooks and goblins and demons and things that go bump in the night. Nature was God's *good* creation, and therefore nothing to be afraid of. Because of this belief, we were now free to investigate nature and to use its desacralized reliability for our own purposes. And in this way Christianity undermined superstition and laid the philosophical foundations necessary for the rise of modern science and technology.

And—my goodness gracious!—how modern science and technology rose. And along with them, something else rose— namely, our confidence in ourselves. And as soon as we obtained this confidence, we felt we had all we needed to chuck the gloomy old God of fear and damnation and make a fresh start. We would throw him down and elevate our own capabilities to the level of godhood. Now we *really* had someone we could look up to and believe in. "The man upstairs" now would no longer be God but only—"Sid"!

ZIGGY

3

And this is exactly what most of Western civilization did. It began believing only in itself and having faith only in its own dreams. It became overwhelmingly *humanistic*. But in getting rid of God we lost something absolutely essential to humanity—and to humanism as well, if humanism is not quickly to become viciously inhumane. We lost our understanding or sense of an ultimate "why" in life. At first we Westerners scarcely noticed this loss of "why" or meaning. We were so busy fighting—and generally winning—the materialistic and scientific and technological battles of "how?" that the question of "why?" was about the last thing we wanted to be bothered with:

HAGAR THE HORRIBLE

But people can't go on fighting for long without some reason or meaning or ultimate purpose *for* fighting. And here's why: if there is no God and no life *after* death, then life itself *cannot* have an ultimate purpose or meaning or "why." If all of life finally ends in death, then what difference does anything *finally* make? What purpose does all of our struggling *finally* serve? When all of life is over and reduced to nothing by the ultimate victory of the grave— never to rise again—what will all of it have meant? What ultimate significance will all of life have had? In this case isn't Shakespeare's Macbeth right?

Life's but . . . a tale
Told by an idiot, full of sound and fury,
Signifying nothing [V, v].

Just like Hägar in the above cartoon, all of us can get carried away for a while by the exhilaration of the fight and conquering new worlds. But just as soon as we stop to consider the final futility of all our fighting—and even the futility of "winning," when finally *everything* is defeated by death, "the last enemy" (1 Cor. 15:26)—then we'll begin to resemble Hägar in *this* cartoon:

HAGAR THE HORRIBLE

This is how *atheism* produces *nihilism*—or belief in practically nothing at all (*nihil*, "nothing"). For if there is no God, said Dostoevsky, then "everything is permitted." And not only does anything go, but also the very *worst* is encouraged. Because if there is no God and immortality, then life's much too short to think about much of anything except "eat, drink and be merry, for tomorrow we die":

ANDY CAPP

Italian film director Federico Fellini has this to say:

People who can no longer believe in a "better tomorrow" logically tend to behave with a desperate egotism. They are preoccupied with protecting, brutally if necessary, those little personal gains, one's little body, one's little sensual appetites. . . . A world dominated by insecurity toward the future [is] thus a life of pure biological reaction—a life of mice, with the ferociousness, the greed, the atrocious existence of mice.[1]

And so it's true that the Western world, being largely atheistic, has now followed atheism's inevitable downward path to becoming largely a race of nihilistic mice. Nothing much is believed in any more except saving our own skins and giving these skins pleasure. But of course the momentary gratification of our skins doesn't really satisfy the deep hunger all people have for believing that finally their lives *do* mean something. Even though our atheism tells us that Macbeth is right, all of us desperately *want* to believe in our own significance—to believe that our lives do *not* "signify nothing":

We will need, however, something far greater than ourselves to convince us of our own significance. When we say "I"—or "Humankind!"— in a very loud voice, we still haven't said "God."

The Religion of Outer Space

First things first. When we say "The Religion of Outer Space," what do we mean by "religion"? Here's a definition of religion that comes from a specifically Christian orientation, and it's the definition I'll be using: *Religion is a do-it-yourself answer to the question of life's meaning.*

Actually, there are *two* ways we can "do" this answer ourselves. But in this first chapter I want to discuss only one of these ways. And that is—we can *dream up* this answer all by ourselves.

This has always been a very handy and popular approach for solving the question of life's meaning. Either we ourselves can dream up some scheme for ultimate meaning or truth for our lives and then do everything possible to convince ourselves that this self-made concoction is really true, or we can simply become believers in a belief that *someone else* has already dreamed up. But in both of these cases, people themselves have created the belief. "Religion" is usually something that *people themselves start.* It's the easiest thing in the world to do, and why anyone would give courses in how to do it is beyond me:

INSIDE WOODY ALLEN

"Of all man's presumptions," writes German theologian Friedrich Gogarten,

that which is commonly known as religion is the most monstrous. For it is the presumption of seeking to bridge over from opposite to opposite, from creator to creature, and to do so by starting from the creature.[2]

A "religion," then, is like our dreams. It's a people-produced illusion. It's the product of our own wishful thinking or *day*dreaming. Religion starts with the attempts of our imaginations to cope with reality—a reality in which the clock is quickly running out for all of us and life tends to be just one rude awakening after another:

ZIGGY

9

This is why the Christian faith claims *not* to be a "religion." Or, to put it another way, Christianity claims to be the only *true* religion. Christian faith claims *it* wasn't dreamed up by anybody. It claims to represent an actual historical and unique encounter—the encounter of a people with the only *eternal* reality—a reality that really exists and comes to us from quite outside ourselves and our world.

But, the Christian faith believes, as long as people haven't had this encounter of this totally different kind, the encounter with God through Christ, they'll still go on *needing* this encounter and will still go on searching for it. In fact, they need this encounter so desperately that in the meantime it becomes extremely easy for them to believe in *any* religion—that is, in any of their own self-made interpretations of reality, regardless of how far-out and obviously self-manufactured this wishful thinking might be. "Religion" is like the tricks our *minds* play on us just because of a deeper want and need in our *hearts*. In *A Midsummer Night's Dream,* Shakespeare describes the origin and tricks of religion's dream in this way:

Such tricks hath strong imagination,
That if it would but apprehend some joy,
It comprehends some bringer of that joy [V, i].

Well said. It works about like this:

MOMMA

As we have said, an *atheistic* people will sooner or later become a *nihilistic* people. But now we go one step farther: a nihilistic people will very quickly become a *religious* people.[3] That is, nihilists will soon be forced to see all sorts of imaginary escapes from the demeaning, demoralizing, and deadening pointlessness of their lives—the pointlessness of their own treadmills or "ditches" to oblivion—when there is no God and therefore no Ultimate to give the trouble of living an ultimate point or purpose or meaning.

BEETLE BAILEY

Now here's another point that's important to understand: It often seems contradictory for the Bible to talk about the original or basic sinfulness of people—or "man" (to use the word *man* as it refers to us all); and yet, at the same time, for the Bible to say that "God made man in his own image" (Gen. 9:6). But properly understood both of these ways of speaking are pointing to the same truth—

namely, people's (or "man's") *built-in need* for the one God who
alone can properly fit and fill "man's" originally empty heart. Saint
Augustine expressed both aspects of this truth in a marvelously clear
and concise way when he wrote, "Our hearts are formed for Thee,
O Lord, and are empty until they find their fulfillment in thee."

In other words, God has created us with his image *in us;* we are
created in such a way that our hearts are originally an empty form or
image that *con*forms exactly to the form or image of God. But this
image of God in our hearts is originally only an *empty* form or image.
Our hearts are originally formed like closed locks that only one key,
God himself, can properly fit and unlock.

"Original sin" simply means that we all originate in life as locks
looking for this lost key. Originally and at heart we are all like hungry,
empty forms that can only be completely and satisfactorily full-filled
by one thing—God himself.

And because Christ, as the New Testament tells us, "is the image
of the invisible God" (Col. 1:15), this means that all of us have within
us, originally and at heart, a "Christ-shaped vacuum." Here is a
picture of Everyman and Everywoman:

We know this is Everyman and Everywoman because we see them Everywhere. If we let "X" stand for Christ, this would mean that Everyman and Everywoman are created like *this* and are looking for *this* kind of key:

Everyman and Everywoman are empty and restless until they are unlocked and made free from this emptiness and restlessness by the only key that can fit and fulfill and free their hearts—Christ himself. This, for instance, is what Jesus meant when he said "the truth will make you free" (John 8:32). Freedom in Christ is the rest and fulfillment and "freedom" we experience when Christ is in us.

John Calvin, one of the great Protestant Reformers, once said that the human mind is a permanent factory of idols. And by now we should have some idea of why this is true. Because of the deep restlessness of our hearts without Christ, our hearts—until they find their rest in Christ—will constantly attempt to fulfill or unlock themselves with all sorts of keys having *incorrect* forms or images. This is what "sin" means. At root, sin is simply looking for God—or ultimate hope—in all the wrong places. And of course all of these "wrong places," from the Christian point of view, are also what is meant by "idols" or "false gods" or "religions." This is why God's Number One Commandment was from the beginning and still is: "You shall have no gods [or keys] except me" (Exod. 20:3, JB).

But now here's an additional point that's crucial to our discussion: Because the locks of our hearts are so desperate to get themselves unlocked and freed, *improper keys* (or idols or religions or false gods) will often be jammed into these locks with a force that can cause these keys to take on some of the actual contours of the only *correct* key—God and/or Christ himself. Our unconscious need for Christ is so strong that even our false gods will sometimes begin to resemble Christ. This resemblance of our idols to Christ will often be only a twisted or distorted or inverted likeness to Christ. But nevertheless a certain visible, unintended correspondence will usually appear between Christ and our false religions or false gods.

Mircea Eliade, one of the world's foremost authorities on the history of religions, has written that

a cultural fashion is immensely significant, no matter what its objective value may be; the success of certain ideas or ideologies reveals to us the spiritual and existential situation of all those for whom these ideas or ideologies constitute a kind of soteriology.[4]

Now one of the best examples of a present-day "cultural fashion" that is certainly successful, significant, and "soteriological" (offering salvation) is what we can call "The Religion of Outer Space." How successful, significant, and salvation-offering is it? Cathy, here, gives us some idea:

CATHY

Space fantasy or "science fiction" may never even mention anything "religious" in the ordinary sense of the word. But whenever this fiction tries to help people find ultimate meaning for their lives, then it is—by definition—*religious*. As a religious fiction it will often display a very sensitive and accurate intuition of what all people are basically hungering and thirsting for. And insofar as it understands *Christ* as the answer to this hunger and thirst, then it's an expression of the *Christian* "religion." But even when this fiction *doesn't* understand Christ as the fulfillment of these needs, it still can bear an unintentional, unconscious, almost predictable resemblance to Christ. Just because of the genuineness, the sincerity, and the forcefulness of the questions behind it, the answers of "The Religion of Outer Space" will draw closer and closer to Christ.

In 1979 *Newsweek* reported:

People can croak, "Entertainment! Entertainment!" until they're blue in the face. The fact remains that films like "Close Encounters of the Third Kind," "Superman," and even "Star Wars" have become jerry-built substitutes for the great myths and rituals of belief, hope and redemption that cultures used to shape before mass secular society took over.[5]

Obviously, a lot of modern space fantasy *is* merely entertainment. On the other hand, as Shoe's "Perfesser" can tell us, a lot of it is much more than this. Science fiction's best representatives do indeed contain "mind-expanding, heavy *philosophy*"; they *can* help us examine our mundane earthbound problems from a fresh, original viewpoint. But then it's also true—a lot of science fiction *is* just "dumb junk."

SHOE

Science fiction appeals to us chiefly because of these two components—*science* and *fiction*. It appeals to us because it would seem to be based on a type of knowledge we already trust—namely, science, and the ability of science to solve our most important problems. But it also appeals to us because it's fiction. For even though scientific truth has promised to be the new savior of humankind, this truth is still a long way from making good on this promise. Modern scientific "advances" could easily be the means by which we all meet our doom. Therefore reality as we know it still

16

leaves us unsatisfied and yearning for a new heaven and new earth. Hence our need for fiction.

ZIGGY

The grass always looks greener on the other side of the cosmos.

2

2001: A Space Odyssey and the Religion of Atheistic Humanism

There's a science fiction classic that stands as an important forerunner to the three films mentioned by *Newsweek*—namely, *2001: A Space Odyssey.* This film furnishes an empty, black sky of bleak hopelessness against which more recent efforts can be seen as twinkling stars of hope. *2001: A Space Odyssey* represents the dark brooding question in response to which *Close Encounters, Superman, Star Wars,* and *E.T.* are attempts to move toward an answer—an answer stronger and more satisfying than the one suggested by *2001.* Stanley Kubrick, the film director, and Arthur C. Clarke, the science fiction writer, were the collaborating creators of *2001;* and in 1968 this is how Kubrick expressed the *question* that is behind *2001:*

Our ability, unlike the other animals, to conceptualize our own end creates tremendous psychic strains within us; whether we like to admit it or not, in each man's chest a tiny ferret of fear at this ultimate knowledge gnaws away at his ego and his sense of purpose. We're fortunate, in a way, that our body, and the fulfillment of its needs and functions, plays such an imperative role in our lives; this physical shell creates a buffer between us and the mind-paralyzing realization that only a few years of existence separate birth from death. If man really sat back and thought about his impending termination, and his terrifying insignificance and aloneness in the cosmos, he would surely go mad, or succumb to a numbing sense of futility. Why, he might ask himself, should he bother to write a great symphony, or strive to make a living, or even to love another, when he is no more than a momentary microbe on a dust mote whirling through the unimaginable immensity of space?

Those of us who are forced by their own sensibilities to view their lives in this perspective—who recognize that there is no purpose they can comprehend and that amidst a countless myriad of stars their existence goes unknown and unchronicled—can fall prey all too easily to the ultimate anomie . . . . But even for those who lack the sensitivity to more than vaguely comprehend their transience and their triviality, this inchoate awareness robs life of meaning and purpose; it's why "the mass of men lead lives of quiet desperation," why so many of us find our lives as absent of meaning as our deaths.

The world's religions, for all their parochialism, did supply a kind of consolation for this great ache; but as clergymen now pronounce the death of God and . . . "the sea of faith" recedes around the world with a "melancholy, long, withdrawing roar," man has no crutch left on which to lean—and no hope, however irrational, to give purpose to his existence. This shattering recognition of our mortality is at the root of far more mental illness than I suspect even psychiatrists are aware.

The interviewer then asked Kubrick to answer his own question. "If life is so purposeless," he said, "do you feel that it's worth living?" And Kubrick's reply is essentially the same answer that is expressed parabolically in *2001.* It is the answer that "man" must pull himself up by his own bootstraps. It is the "answer" of *atheistic humanism:*

Yes, for those of us who manage somehow to cope with our mortality. The very meaninglessness of life forces man to create his own meaning. Children, of course, begin life with an untarnished sense of wonder, a capacity to experience total joy at something as simple as the greenness of a leaf; but as they grow older, the awareness of death and decay begins to impinge on their consciousness and subtly erode their joie de vivre, their idealism—and their assumption of immortality. As a child matures, he sees death and pain everywhere about him, and begins to lose faith in faith and in the ultimate goodness of man. But if he's reasonably strong—and lucky—he can emerge from this twilight of the soul into a rebirth of life's élan.

Both because of and in spite of his awareness of the
meaninglessness of life, he can forge a fresh sense of
purpose and affirmation. He may not recapture the
same pure sense of wonder he was born with, but he can
shape something far more enduring and sustaining.
The most terrifying fact about the universe is not that
it is hostile but that it is indifferent; but if we can
come to terms with this indifference and accept the
challenges of life within the boundaries of death—
however mutable man may be able to make them—our
existence as a species can have genuine meaning and
fulfillment. However vast the darkness, we must supply
our own light.[1]

In case anyone missed the beautiful little contradiction in Kubrick's "answer" here, it goes like this: "In spite of man's awareness of the meaninglessness of life . . . his life can have genuine meaning." A neat trick. Fortunately, though, Kubrick's a better film director than a philosopher.

It's no accident that Kubrick's *2001* opens with the pomp and heroic stanzas of Richard Strauss's tone poem *Also Sprach Zarathustra*—Strauss's "homage to the genius of Nietzsche"[2]— because Friedrich Nietzsche's book *Thus Spake Zarathustra* contains his famous proclamation of "the death of God." Nietzsche didn't feel that *he* was responsible for God's death, of course. He was simply announcing something that he believed had already taken place in most modern people's thinking. People were scarcely conscious of this revolutionary modern assumption, Nietzsche believed, but its effects would soon be felt far and wide and deeply throughout the world. And in this last respect at least, Nietzsche was correct.

The revolution brought on by God's death (or people no longer believing in God) would be that people themselves would have to be their own god. A Jewish proverb tells us that a man is not fully a man until his father dies. Well now, with the death of our *heavenly* father, "men" will have fully come of age. Now we will have to be the master of our own fate and captain of our own soul. We will now determine our own destiny and give meaning to our own existence and "create our own decalogues," as Nietzsche put it. With this newfound freedom from God's tutelage and restraint, "men" will now pull themselves up to new, undreamed-of heights, becoming "supermen" in their mastery of the world, Nietzsche believed. Here's a picture of a bust of Nietzsche as it's being admired by one of his ideological offspring.

But Nietzsche's philosophy of God's death and the superman's birth was itself a bust, as disciple Hitler so dramatically demonstrated. For, as we have said, without God and human immortality, life finally becomes only a "here today—gone tomorrow" affair, and can only mean—if it can mean anything—getting yours while the getting's good. And never mind what you have to do to get yours. Without God around, we make up our own rules. Since a brief time is all we have before we're all swallowed up by the grave, instant selfish gratification will naturally become the order of the day.

Strange to say, people can still fall for Nietzsche's philosophy of the death of God without seeing its disastrous down-to-earth implications just around the corner. Like Nietzsche himself, they can believe that God's demise will bring about better things. And Arthur C. Clarke and Stanley Kubrick are two such people. Beware of bad philosophers bearing good entertainment.

Spanish philosopher Miguel de Unamuno once said that all human questions are overshadowed by one question: Are we alone in the universe or not? Unamuno was concerned about whether there was a God in the universe, because he knew that if there wasn't, then the whole universe would finally be no more than the pits. But Clarke and Kubrick would interpret this statement differently. Since, as they believe, God is dead and therefore humanity is now its own god, they want to know if we gods—or people—are the only *living beings* in the universe. They hope not, because this would give them a stronger sense of cosmic loneliness than they care to live with. Something about like this:

MISS PEACH

The *Miss Peach* comic strip is ripe with the wisdom of many philosophers, and one of them, Arthur, can rephrase Unamuno's question in this way:

MISS PEACH

Clarke and Kubrick would tell us that *no one* is in charge here. The universe is simply a clocklike, impersonal mechanism, utterly blind and unfeeling and indifferent to people and their problems. No one's in charge. The universe just is. Therefore we can look only to ourselves for help and hope. And of course this is "human-ism" or the deification of humanity. Human self-deification also explains why humanism will always be a popular idea. Naturally we humans like to think the best of ourselves. So when some flattering philosophy tells us that we ourselves are divine, so much the better. We humans like humanism for the same reason this man likes this portrait of himself:

"By George, I like that! Yes, I like that very much!"

In Clarke and Kubrick's view of things, so well dramatized in *2001*, "man" is on a kind of Nietzschean evolutionary trip to becoming a superman—"the Ultimate Trip," the film calls it. In *2001* this evolution is sparked by an alien intelligence that, in the form of a mysterious giant monolith, nudges a prehistoric race of apes into the direction of intelligence. And so these apes eventually evolve into people. Later on, when people have developed sufficiently, they find the monolith on the moon where it's been placed by the alien intelligence. Its discovery on the moon signals to the higher beings that humankind

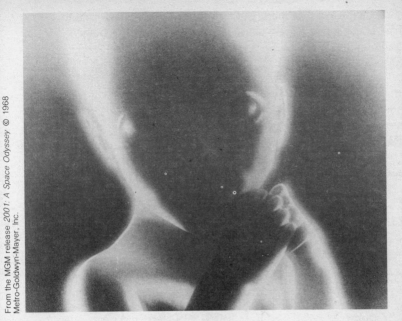

has now reached the capability of space travel. And so from the moon it would seem to be easy enough for the monolith to lead them to Jupiter, the source of the alien intelligence; and from Jupiter one of the space travelers actually makes it through Jupiter's "star gate" and then on "beyond the infinite." There, beyond the infinite, the space traveler is transformed into some kind of superhuman "star-child, ' who is then sent back to the earth to take charge of it. The star-child, brooding over the world, is unsure at first just what he'll do with it. "But," as we are told at the conclusion of Clarke's novel, "he would think of something." Now supermen are in charge.

Now this space odyssey is certainly a fascinating tale or modern myth, but there are important questions that Clarke and Kubrick never get around to taking seriously. Most important among these questions is: What's the point? Why so much effort to take so long a trip when presumably death is still going to have the last word over all these efforts anyway? Even star-children, just like stars, are finally subject to death and decay in a godless and coldly indifferent universe. But maybe it's a good thing if we rush to reach the stars.

Because if we *do* get there, maybe we'll then finally have time to think about that important question that never seems to bother Clarke and Kubrick:

ANDY CAPP

In getting rid of God, modern people felt they were finally freeing themselves for noble causes and great accomplishments in the universe. *2001* is a good example of this humorless, humanistic, self-important intoxication. But people are now beginning to realize that in cutting themselves loose from their special God-relationship, they've cut away the very basis for believing that their roles and accomplishments and causes have any special significance or meaning or nobility at all. In a godless universe, people are no more significant than—weeds!

B.C.

Without God and immortality, the entire story of humankind when all is said and done—indeed the entire secret of the universe—finally makes no more sense nor is any more meaningful than this:

FRANK AND ERNEST

And so much for *2001* and its religion of atheistic humanism.

Visions Drawing Closer to Christ:
Close Encounters of the Third Kind and *Superman*

Close Encounters

2001 first appeared in 1968 and was typical of a lot of the naively optimistic talk we were then hearing about humankind and its God-like powers and possibilities. But in only a few short years we've been able to see through this shallow optimism into the deep "black hole" that it was built over. Perhaps it would be more accurate to call it an optimism we've *fallen* through, because this shallow humanism that we stood on was only a thin sheet of ice covering the infinitely deep ocean of meaninglessness and despair when there is no God. In any case we've been forced to turn back to the *human* problem. For how can we ever hope to conquer "outer space" when we can't even solve the more basic problems that we have within and among ourselves?

B.C.

The Gospel from Outer Space

While it lasted, it was fun and fascinating to contemplate the possibilities of intelligent life in outer space. But this luxury has now been interrupted by a disturbing lack of intelligent life closer to home:

ZIGGY

The question about whether we are the only life in the universe tends to become unreal, academic, and forgotten when struggling with the very real, personal, won't-go-away loneliness we can feel even among one another and even in spite of our best attempts to overcome this loneliness:

MISS PEACH

We can't understand it and therefore we can hardly stand it. Every problem seems capable of being solved except the human problem. A famous scientist—Albert Einstein—put it this way:

The real problem is in the hearts of men . . . . It is easier to change the nature of plutonium than man's evil spirit.[1]

30

A famous Christian theologian—Dietrich Bonhoeffer—said it like this:

Man is again thrown back on himself. He has managed to deal with everything, only not with himself. He can insure against everything, only not against man. In the last resort it all turns on man.[2]

Our collective *self*-confidence and *self*-admiration have taken a serious nosedive. The romantic idea of visiting the far reaches of *outer* space has been rudely sobered up by our seeming inability to deal effectively with the more mundane problems of human *inner* space:

BEETLE BAILEY

The Gospel from Outer Space

One thing is sure: If we're to reach *2001*'s rosy vision by *that* date, we'd better get moving. At least some of the forecasts for *1999* certainly aren't all that beautiful:

BROOM–HILDA

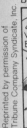

GAYLORD, DO YOU THINK WORLD CONDITIONS WILL BE BETTER OR WORSE BY 1999?

I BELIEVE BY 1999 THERE WILL BE WIDESPREAD POVERTY, RAMPANT CRIME, AND RAGING IMMORALITY.

IS THAT BETTER OR WORSE?

So we've now reached the point where we feel we need big help in a big hurry. Therefore, instead of placing our hopes in visiting outer space in the distant future, a hope reflected in *2001,* our here-and-now situation has become so desperate that we're now dreaming of outer space *visiting us*. What we now want is a "close encounter" or "a way" out *right now*.

Back in the days of Orson Welles's famous radio program "The War of the Worlds" (1938), we were terrified by the idea of outer-space aliens taking over the earth. But now it would seem that this is an idea whose time has come.

FRANK AND ERNEST

This is why Steven Spielberg's dazzling cinematic hymn to flying saucers, *Close Encounters of the Third Kind,* is so much a sign of the times. The giant "mother ship" of *Close Encounters* is a dream machine that delivers exactly what we now feel we need: a quick fix. We need a once-and-for-all revelation to come from *outside in;* a revelation that will come down to us producing meaning, direction, and unity for our lives; a revelation that will quickly fill the sterile, empty vacuums of our hearts with faith, hope, and charity.

But *Close Encounters* is more than just another sign of our *particular* time. It is actually an extremely significant religious film— and book—that points to the deepest questions and answers of *all* time. As such it is a far more *truly* religious film than 99 percent of the overtly "religious" schlock Hollywood has produced in the past. *Close Encounters* is a beautiful modern-day parable, the story of a space visitation that bears uncanny resemblances to the very visitation all of us need, the visitation of Christ into our darkened hearts. No doubt these resemblances are unintended by Spielberg, the story's creator. But again, this only points to how many of the "keys" manufactured by a society will, because of that society's great need, take on surprising and unexpected resemblances to the correct key—Christ.

From the very opening of his story, Spielberg seems to have a high-strung sensitivity to the spiritual wasteland that characterizes humankind's current condition. A subtitle tells us that it is the "Present Day" as the film opens on a blinding desert sandstorm. The scene quickly switches to the darkness of night where there is, among other ominous bits and pieces, an argument among the technicians who manage a shorted-out power station. Early in the film Roy Neary, an employee of the power company and the film's hero, pores over maps and gropes in his truck through the darkened boondocks, searching for the power failure's source. Neary finds that source, for later that night he has astonishing encounters of the first kind—a "sighting"—and the second kind—"physical evidence"— of a UFO. And from that point on, Neary is a person *possessed.*

For it seems the UFO has implanted in Neary, and in a small group of other people it has encountered, a mysterious image. This "scooped out'" form in these "invited" few turns out to be the image of Devil's Tower, which in actual fact is a huge, unique geological formation in Wyoming. But at first Neary and the others in whom this image has been fixed have only a vague feeling for what this strange form inside them could look like or mean. Consequently, they find themselves constantly attempting to make some kind of outward representation of this haunting inward "vision." And as soon as they get it, as soon as they recognize this restless form inside them as the image of Devil's Tower, these "nobodies" from all over the country then converge at the same time at just that location. The scientific community has been tipped off in advance and is already waiting at Devil's Tower. But interestingly enough, it isn't until Roy Near-y and his little band of fellow "nobodies" draw near that the enormous mother ship also draws near in all its overwhelming power and glory. The space ship is obviously all-powerful, the radiant "aliens" inside it are obviously super-knowing and all-loving, and Roy Neary is then overjoyed to be taken on board along with twelve other earthlings; they are whisked away on the giant flying saucer, and then presumably everybody—all of humankind—lives much more happily ever after. The End.

It's an absolutely fascinating tale that Spielberg spins for us in his novel and film. And the parallels between *Close Encounters* and the Christian faith are almost too many to try to list—parallels both in the way it asks questions and in the answers it suggests.

For instance, I've mentioned the dramatized spiritual need with which Spielberg begins his story. Roy Neary's wife tells him, "I'm so starved for something to happen" (p. 32).[3] Neary himself, like Snoopy, just wants to know "what's going on" (p. 125). When Neary is asked by one of the scientists what he expects to find at Devil's Tower,

Neary struggled to formulate a reply. What the hell was he doing here? "The answer," he said, at last. "That's not crazy, is it?" [p. 191].

When he attempts to explain his quest to his children, Neary tells them,

"It's like when you know the music but you just don't remember the words? I don't know how to say it, what I'm thinking ... but ... this means something ... this is important" [p. 143].

People's built-in quest for meaning and their looking for the lost key for which they were made, is central to the story of *Close*

Encounters. "Everybody has a secret wish," Neary tells his kids. "I can't explain it. All I can say is that it's stronger than anything else" (p. 170). This hollowed-out, hungry wish implanted in Neary and in his fellow nobodies is a marvelous parallel to what we've been saying about the hollowed-out, hungry image of. God originally implanted in all people. And just as we said that this empty image can only be fulfilled by something from outside ourselves and we compared this something to the one key that *alone* can unlock a particular lock, likewise in *Close Encounters* "the mountain was the key" (p. 204). Christians see Christ as the unique, one-of-a-kind key to the knowledge of God. And in *Close Encounters*

the Tower stood alone, something so one-of-a-kind that Neary felt a chill across his shoulders at the thought he had been able to reproduce it in sculpture without even knowing it existed [p. 183].

This is also why it's so interesting that in *Close Encounters* so much emphasis is placed on finding the single, exact time-and-place *point*—the "coordinates"—of what it understands to be the most revealing and important event in all history. Because in the Bible precisely the same kind of "zeroing-in" process is also taking place. All of the biblical writers—both Old Testament and New—gather around, face, and point with increasing clarity to what T. S. Eliot called "the still point of the turning world"—namely, Christ, who was also lifted up on a kind of "devil's tower."

When Neary starts getting near to the place of revelation he isn't frightened. He tells the woman he's in love with, "I've got to get closer." And in *Close Encounters* we also have come much closer to the Christian revelation than perhaps we bargained for. When Neary first sees Devil's Tower on television and recognizes it to be the fulfillment of the empty image inside him, he exclaims

"Jesus!" ... *In one jump he knelt before the television screen [p. 163].*

And when the "mother ship" finally appears over Devil's Tower, the scientist who is in charge of the project can only murmur, "Oh, my God!"

Keys resembling the Key—but a resemblance probably produced more by need and unconscious memory than by conscious intention. On the one hand, the *Close Encounters'* theme song of "Wishing upon a Star," a distant hope in the dark that something improbable *will* happen; on the other hand, a witness in the daylight of history to an event that's *already* happened.

LOCHER

Spielberg evidently really believes in flying saucers.[4] But I must confess to my own skepticism. Carl Jung made a careful study of the UFO phenomenon. And in a letter written in 1957 to a man in Springfield, Illinois, Jung said, "As it is questionable in how far UFOs are physical facts, it is indubitable that they are psychological facts. They have a very definite and very meaningful psychology."[5] And although Jung remained scientifically noncommittal in his conclusions about the *physical* existence of UFOs, his 1954 description of their psychological origin matches my feelings about their *total* origin.

We have a bleak, shallow rationalism that offers stones instead of bread to the emotional and spiritual hungers of the world. The logical result is an insatiable hunger for anything extraordinary. If we add to this the great defeat of human reason, daily demonstrated in the newspapers and rendered even more menacing by the incalculable dangers of the hydrogen bomb, the picture that unfolds before us is one of universal spiritual distress, comparable to the situation at the beginning

of our era or to chaos that followed A.D. *1000, or the
upheavals at the turn of the fifteenth century. It is
therefore not surprising if, as the old chroniclers
report, all sorts of signs and wonders appear in the
sky, or if miraculous intervention, where human efforts
have failed, is expected from heaven. Our saucer
sightings can be found in many reports that go back to
antiquity, though not, it would seem, with the same
overwhelming frequency. But then, the possibility of
destruction on a global scale, which has been given
into the hands of our so-called politicians, did not
exist in those days.*

 *McCarthyism and the influence it has exerted are
evidence of the deep and anxious apprehensions of the
American public. Therefore most of the signs in the
skies will be seen in North America.*[6]

 I think it's also interesting to notice *when* the flying saucer
phenomenon began to occur in the twentieth century. It was
immediately following the Second World War—probably the most
traumatic experience humankind has ever gone through, with its
millions slain, its atomic bombs, and its Holocaust. In other words, I
wouldn't be surprised if there were strong connections between our
need for a close encounter of the third kind and our close encounter
with the Third Reich. In any case, a war like this can certainly give
rise to one other psychologically attractive aspect to outer space
intervention. And that's the ability such an intervention might have to
unify everybody in the face of a common friend or foe.

BEETLE BAILEY

Fortunately, however, it's not necessary to wait for some outer
space breakthrough before we can all become fellow human beings.
Christianity believes that something of this kind of "intervention" has

already occurred. In Christ, our older brother, we're much more than fellow human beings. We're all revealed to be one another's brothers and sisters, and children of the same loving heavenly Father. Whether we know it or not. The important thing then, of course, is that we know it.

Anyway, even if we were to experience a close encounter of the scientifically verifiable kind, there's no guarantee that it would be all that helpful:

KELLY AND DUKE

Superman I

MARLETTE

There is a man who was sent to earth by his father, was raised in humble circumstances and since he was not of this world dwelt among men an outsider..... But his was a special destiny...... By dedicating his unique gifts to the service of truth and justice he stood for the oppressed, the meek, the afflicted, the powerless...... for all of humanity...... This is *not* Him.

MARLETTE
THE CHARLOTTE OBSERVER

One of the things this Marlette cartoon does, of course, is to show us very briefly and clearly some of the many parallels between Christ and the Superman of the movie *(Superman I)*. Because in its use of traditional Christian imagery and familiar biblical language—including some practically direct steals from Scripture—*Superman I* is about as subtle as a kick in the teeth.

In the opening scenes, as the planet Krypton begins to disintegrate, Superinfant's parents wrap him in red, white, and blue swaddling clothes and lay him in an unearthly manger. Superman's father, Jor-El, tells him:

All that I have I bequeath you, my son. You'll carry me inside you all the days of your life. You will see my life through yours, and yours through mine. The son becomes the father and the father the son.[7]

At this point the script sounds as if it might have been ghost-written by the author of the Gospel of John.

The only begotten son then becomes a new type of ''star-child''

40

as he escapes Krypton in a spaceship and travels through space and time to reach the earth at a preordained place. And just in case anyone hasn't gotten the point by this time, Superchild, upon his arrival, gives us one more less-than-subtle hint as he opens his arms wide to suggest a miniature Christ.

Soon the eighteen-year-old Superboy is compelled by a mysterious force to journey to an Arctic wasteland where he is received into the brilliantly lighted "Fortress of Solitude," an "impenetrable secret sanctuary" complete with baptismal waters. Superboy then spends "literally years in the Fortress mastering his super-powers and communing with the image of his father in preparation for his lifelong war against evil."[8] In this retreat to the wilderness, Superboy is instructed by "the voice and image of his long-dead father, Jor-El," who tells Superboy, "They only need the light to show them the way. For this reason, and this reason only, I have sent you, my only son." At age thirty, the fully matured Superman returns to the daily world of the sin-darkened planet "to fight for truth, justice and the American way."

Thus begins Superman's continuing series of super-exploits.

In our revival of *Superman,* just as in *Close Encounters,* we've come a long way from *2001*'s optimistic view of *ourselves* as potential Nietzschean "supermen," traveling through space and conquering the universe. For in *Superman* and in *Close Encounters,* we're willing to settle for super-aliens *coming to us,* rather than our going to them or becoming super-aliens ourselves. But in *Superman* we've even made another concession: we're willing to settle for the Superman of *fiction.* We're ready to find consolation in something totally and obviously mythological rather than letting ourselves suffer too much disappointment when something *real* from space doesn't show up. This is why we'll always "need" Superman. Not only is the *real* not getting the job done, but it doesn't even seem to hold out much hope in that direction. As a matter of fact, "the real" has now become ominously threatening.

HI AND LOIS

So in Superman, our great need has again forced us to conjure up an image that draws closer to Christ—Christ being the fulfillment we're *really* looking for. Because if Superman doesn't teach us anything else, he at least points to the built-in need we all have for our deliverer to be a *single "man."*

This need is expressed in the biblical messianic hope that God would send his Messiah in the form of a single human being, a person just like us, who could speak to us and show us, through *human* words and deeds, the way to the truth and the life. The Messiah would not be some sort of overwhelming and dazzling space deity, as in *2001* or *Close Encounters;* but instead the Messiah would be one of us, our friend with whom we could walk and talk and share human feelings. So there is a significant resemblance of Superman to Christ in the "man" part. But an essential difference is in the "super."

Jesus was very cautious in using the "super-powers" of his Father, although he obviously could have at any time. "Do you think that I cannot appeal to my Father, and he will at once send me more than twelve legions of angels?" he asked one of his followers (Matt. 26:53). But why was this the case? Why did Christ generally refrain from this kind of outwardly obvious use of supernatural power?

It's because of who Christ *was.* Christ was *himself* the decisive, normative, authoritative, absolutely unique, once-and-for-all revelation of God to humankind. For this reason Christ *himself* is to be believed in and is the sole object of Christ-ian belief. And this means, logically, that if we follow Christ because of certain "signs" or proofs that he has given us, then in this case we're not followers of *this humble man* at all. We're only followers of or believers in signs and proofs. Therefore Christ could say, "An evil and adulterous generation seeks for a sign" (Matt. 12:39, 16:4), adultery referring here to *spiritual* infidelity.

This is also why belief in something like Superman is always so much easier and, for just this reason, will always tend to be more popular. Belief in Superman requires nothing from us. All we have to do is to see him (or something like him) in action—with his "signs" and "proofs." In this way "belief" is handed to us on a silver platter. It's belief based on what we *already* trust—signs and proofs and seeing with our own eyes. But this is precisely why Christ doesn't let us off so easily and why he rejected the role of a superman. When we confront him, something infinitely greater is required of us— namely, *"faith,* not . . . sight"* (2 Cor. 5:7). The man who stood in front of us and asked, "Who do you say that I am?" (Matt. 16:15) was no superman. He was a humble rabbi, a "meek and lowly" (Matt. 11:29, KJV) shepherd, "the carpenter's son," whose mother and brothers and sisters the people also knew (Matt. 13:55–6). Therefore to believe in *this* man requires a radically deep sacrifice on our parts. That is, we've got to give up what we originally and already trust in if we are to trust only in him. And so ultimately we get no signs or proofs. Otherwise our faith ultimately would be *in* signs or proofs. This is why God did not send our Savior to us in the form of a *super*man, but rather in the form of a *servant*man, a lowly man of sorrows who finally would not even save himself from the torment, the humiliation, the death, of the cross.

When we look back over what we've said about the saviors described in *Close Encounters* and *Superman,* I hope we can now have more appreciation for and insight into the following observations by astronomer Carl Sagan:

> **The interest in UFOs and ancient astronauts seems at**
> **least partly the result of unfulfilled religious needs.**
> **The extraterrestrials are often described as wise,**
> **powerful, benign, human in appearance, and sometimes**
> **they are attired in long white robes. They are very**

much like gods and angels, coming from other planets rather than from heaven, using spaceships rather than wings. There is a little pseudoscientific overlay, but the theological antecedents are clear .... Indeed, a recent British survey suggests that more people believe in extraterrestrial visitations than in God.[9]

When we anxiously search the skies nowadays, what we're really looking for, whether we realize it or not, is God's revelation of himself in Christ. So in a sense, then, it may be that "the religion of outer space" is pointing us in the right direction when it directs our gaze upward. But that's not because it's the religion of outer space that's finally going to help us. Beetle Bailey's Chaplain Stainglass helps us understand what can *really* help:

BEETLE BAILEY

Closer Still to Christ: The *Star Wars* Saga, or "The Gospel According to Saint Lucas"*

Although it will be years before George Lucas completes all of the projected chapters of his marvelous *Star Wars* series, what we've already seen and read is more than enough to convince us that

- *the entire saga should be wonderful and magnificent in scope;*
- *it will be amazingly popular with all-age groups and for ages to come;*
- *it is now and will remain extremely close to the Christian faith in its overall vision and probably in many of its details.*

There should be no need to defend the popularity of the *Star Wars* series. Its popularity is deserved. These are wild, exciting, and imaginatively produced stories. I don't understand how *anyone* could sit through seven straight showings of such a film. In only *one* showing I'm in about the same condition as Beetle Bailey's "Sarge":

BEETLE BAILEY

It's also no surprise that *Star Wars* fans have quickly spotted many analogies between these stories and the Christian faith. A lot of these points of correspondence can reach out and smack a

---

* *Lucas*, by the way, is the Latinized form of *Lukas*, the word used by the original Greek New Testament for *Luke*, as in "The Gospel According to . . ."

45

person in the eye. Darth Vader and the Empire he serves are obviously bigger-than-life symbols for evil on its powerful, forbidding, cosmic scale. But then there are also the many positive symbols or forces for good that are not difficult to recognize. Chief among these is the unseen "Force" itself, which can easily be translated into the biblical word "power": God himself as power (" . . . for thine is . . . the power"), the power of God's Holy Spirit (e.g., Rom. 15:13), and God's fallen or distorted power as it becomes "the power of darkness" (Luke 22:53). Wise and saintly Ben Kenobi certainly fits the role of a Christ-symbol: he instructs Luke Skywalker in the ways of the Force, is then killed in battle with Darth Vader, but then miraculously returns from the dead in a spiritual form and continues to lead Luke in their common war against evil.

The Empire Strikes Back contains striking parallels between the training Yoda gives Luke for becoming a Jedi warrior and basic training in Christianity.

"To become a Jedi," Yoda said gravely, "takes the deepest commitment, the most serious kind" [p. 110].[1]

When Luke replies that he's not afraid, Yoda answers: "Heh, You will be" (p. 111). Later Yoda instructs Luke to go into a "sinister cave" at the base of a mysterious tree that "is strong with the dark side of the Force" (p. 141). "What's in there?" Luke wants to know. "Only what you take with you," Yoda tells him cryptically. When Luke enters the base of the tree, he immediately encounters the looming figure of Darth Vader, and they fall into a duel using their light-sabers. In one powerful stroke Luke severs the Dark Lord's head from his body.

As Luke watched in shocked disbelief, the broken helmet fell aside to reveal, not the unknown, imagined face of Darth Vader, but Luke's own face, looking up at him [p. 144].

As if this weren't enough, it's later revealed in *The Empire* that Darth Vader is actually Luke's own father, harking back to a comment Yoda earlier made about Luke: "Much anger in him . . . . Like his father" (p. 110). Also, Yoda tells Luke that in order to become a Jedi warrior, Luke must forget his "old" standards and measures. "Unlearn, unlearn!" Yoda tells him.

And so, then, the evil tree, "we have met the enemy and he is us," our own origins, our need to first get rid of the "old" person inside us—what could be more imaginative ways of talking about the basic problem of all people as Christianity understands that problem, which is the meaning of the Christian teaching of original sin.

Many of the teachings Ben Kenobi and Yoda give to Luke about "the Force" sound as if they could have been taken directly from the teachings of Jesus. At one point, for instance, the tiny Yoda, using only the power of the invisible Force, lifts Luke's enormous X-wing fighter out of a dense bog and sets it gently on dry land. Luke responds in utter astonishment, "I don't believe it!" And as the book puts it,

"That," Yoda stated emphatically, "is why you fail" [p. 124].

"That" also is extremely close to one of the better-known sayings of Jesus:

If you have faith as a mustard seed, you will say to this mountain, "move from here to there," and it will move. And nothing will be impossible to you [Matt. 17:20].

Luke "silently vowed never to use the word 'impossible' again," the episode concludes (p. 124).

Jesus also teaches his disciples to deal drastically with temptation: "If your right hand causes you to sin," he tells us, "cut it off and throw it away" (Matt. 5:30). And toward the conclusion of *The Empire* we know that Luke is strongly tempted by the seeming futility of being up against the awesome power of evil in Darth Vader. Luke's "spirit was prepared to succumb to his fate," the book tells us. "There was no reason to fight anymore—there was nothing left to believe in" (p. 209). And so perhaps it's no accident that in *The Empire* Luke's right hand is cut off in a final battle with Darth Vader. But Luke's temptation ultimately is overcome and a "new hand" is "skillfully fused to Luke's arm" (p. 213).

The problem of there being "nothing left to believe in," especially for young people, seems to be a central concern for George Lucas, creator of the *Star Wars* series. Lucas seems to be keenly aware that genuine belief—"belief" as opposed to "knowledge"—is a rare commodity these days. No doubt this is why "the Force" is clearly a religious or "belief" symbol, rather than a symbol for scientific knowledge. "Hocus-pocus religions and archaic weapons are no substitute for a good blaster at your side,'' Han Solo sneeringly says of the Force at one point in *Star Wars* (p. 121). So *Star Wars* is obviously just as concerned about today's dearth of belief as this star is:

ZIGGY

In a 1980 newspaper interview, Lucas was asked, "Do you believe that your films contribute to a better world by having characters like Luke and Ben Kenobi with superhuman powers?" And Lucas answered:

Star Wars *was done with that in mind. . . . I feel strongly about the role myths and fairy tales play in setting up young people for the way they're supposed to handle themselves in society. It's the kind of thing psychiatrist Bruno Bettelheim talks about, the importance of childhood. I realized before I did* **Star Wars** *that there was no contemporary fairy tale and that the number of parents who sit down and tell their children fairy tales is dwindling. As families begin to break up, kids are left more to the television and they don't hear bedtime stories. As a result, people are learning their mythology from TV, which makes them very confused because it has no point of view, no sense of morality. It's a very amoral thing and as a result, unless a child has a very strong family life or is involved with the church, there's no anchor to hold on to. So when I developed* **Star Wars** *I did it as a contemporary fairy tale. I think that's one of the reasons it has universal appeal.*

Then the interviewer asked Lucas, "Then *Star Wars* is a morality play?"And Lucas replied:

It's also a psychological tool that children can use to understand the world better and their place in it and how to adjust to that. It's very basic. It's where religion came from. Fairy tales, religion, were all designed to teach man the right way to live and give him a moral anchor.[2]

The introduction to Bruno Bettelheim's book *The Uses of Enchantment* is entitled "The Struggle for Meaning." And in this essay Bettelheim throws additional light on what George Lucas is up to:

There is a widespread refusal to let children know that the source of much that goes wrong in life is due to our very own natures—the propensity of all men for acting aggressively, asocially, selfishly, out of anger and anxiety. Instead, we want our children to believe that, inherently, all men are good. But children know that they are not always good; and often, even when they are, they would prefer not to be. This contradicts what they are told by their parents, and therefore makes the child a monster in his own eyes.

The dominant culture wishes to pretend, particularly where children are concerned, that the dark side of man does not exist, and professes a belief in an optimistic meliorism. . . . "Safe" stories mention neither death nor aging, the limits to our existence, nor the wish for eternal life. The fairy tale, by contrast, confronts the child squarely with the basic human predicaments.

Today children no longer grow up within the security of an extended family, or of a well-integrated community. Therefore, even more than at the times fairy tales were invented, it is important to provide the modern child with images of heroes who have to go out into the world all by themselves and who, although originally ignorant of the ultimate things, find secure places in the world by following their right way with deep inner confidence.

Bettelheim also tells us that "as works of art, fairy tales have many aspects worth exploring" that are "communicated to the child's mind . . . . Fairy tales also abound in religious motifs," he reminds us.[3]

We have seen a few of the *specific* "religious motifs" that are apparently being communicated through the *Star Wars* saga. But I believe the *overall* vision of faith that's being expressed in this series is of much greater significance. For what we receive through these celestial wars, I believe, is a strong witness to an ultimate, unconditional, triumphal "celestial" victory. And it is, I believe, primarily because of this strong note of a joyful optimism, of a complete, final triumph of the good over *all* evil, that the *Star Wars* series has struck such a responsive chord in the hearts of so many. Lucas tells us that he is a "religious person," that "I believe in God and I believe in good."[4] And it is *this* faith, I think, Lucas's implied belief in the final and total victory of the ultimate good as it fights the ultimate battle, that not only gives *Star Wars* a wider popularity but also accounts for its powerful appeal to our deepest yearnings and needs.

The very first words of the series' opening chapter, *Star Wars,* are: "A Long Time Ago . . ." In other words, this is not another science fiction drama set in the future. No, this is the story about a cosmic battle that took place long ago and therefore has *already* been fought and won.

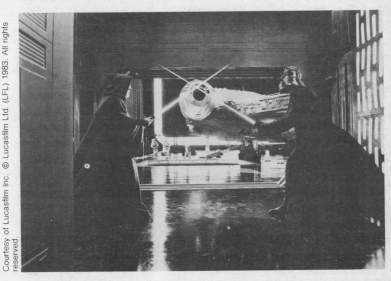

But why should this story about a cosmic victory in the past have such meaning and significance—especially for Christians? Answer: Because this kind of story is also *the* good news of the Christian message, a message that tells us—when it's properly understood— that God has *already* triumphed over *all* of the forces of sin and evil and death and that this victory has been totally won and finished for *all* people—not for just *a few* people or *some* people. No, *this* victory means the *unconditional* surrender of *all* the powers of darkness, and therefore it is a victory the fruits of which will finally come unconditionally to *all* the people. The word "gospel" means "good news." Therefore the gospel according to Luke and the gospel according to Lucas would seem to be virtually the same: "Be not afraid; for behold I bring you good news of a great joy which will come to all the people" (Luke 2:10). If one single soul—even Darth Vader!—is finally excluded from sharing the benefits of God's victory, then God has not been *totally* triumphant. There would still

51

be something apart from God which would be stronger than God and His will. Any being that is finally allowed to defy God is finally victorious over God. But the Bible assures us this will never happen. God will *finally* be "all in all." And this is exactly the way Saint Paul expresses it: "And when all things are thus subject to him, then . . . God will be all in all" (1 Cor. 15:28, NEB).

If God is *not* finally all in all, then this would mean that Christ has been the leader of only a limited or partial rescue operation. And the "good news" would be only a drastically limited or partial "good news"—really more of a *bad* news than good. But like Christ himself, Christians would consign no one to final separation from God. They wish "that *all* men should find salvation and come to know the truth" (1 Tim. 2:4, NEB). Christ and Christians are like Ben Kenobi in the *Star Wars* story:

Kenobi retained values most modern men could have deemed archaic. He would consign no one to the bone-gnawers and gravel-maggots, not even a filthy jawa [p. 88].

Through Christ, Christians know that God is the *all*-loving and *all*-powerful father. Therefore, like their leader, Christ, Christians will also have a good will about the ultimate fate of the "other team."

PEANUTS

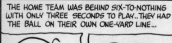

PEOPLE WERE JUMPING UP AND DOWN, AND WHEN THEY KICKED THE EXTRA POINT, THOUSANDS OF PEOPLE RAN OUT ONTO THE FIELD LAUGHING AND SCREAMING! THE FANS AND THE PLAYERS WERE SO HAPPY THEY WERE ROLLING ON THE GROUND AND HUGGING EACH OTHER AND DANCING AND EVERYTHING!

IT WAS FANTASTIC!

HOW DID THE OTHER TEAM FEEL?

PEANUTS

This way of understanding Christianity as a message of triumphant joy and supreme optimism is found in the New Testament itself, of course; and in the history of the church's thinking it has often been called the "dramatic" or "classical" view of the atonement—the "at-one-ment" referring to the exact way in which God and people came together in Christ and are reconciled as "one." "Jesus is victor!" is a slogan often associated with this view—a view that from beginning to end is solidly based on the Bible. For instance Jesus could say:

In the world you will have trouble. But courage! The victory is mine; I have conquered the world [John 16:33, NEB].

But the great Protestant theologian Karl Barth has in recent years probably done the best job of giving renewed and powerful expression to this ancient view of the atonement. Barth can write:

In the resurrection of Jesus Christ the claim is made, according to the New Testament, that God's victory in man's favour in the person of His Son has already been won. Easter is indeed the great pledge of our hope, but simultaneously this future is already present in the Easter message. It is the proclamation of a victory already won. The war is at an end—even though here and there troops are still shooting, because they have not heard anything yet about the capitulation. The game is won, even though the player can still play a few further moves. Actually he is already mated. The clock has run down, even though the pendulum still swings a few times this way and that. It is in this interim space that we are living: the old is past, behold it has all become new. The Easter message tells us that our enemies, sin, the curse and death, are beaten.

Ultimately they can no longer start mischief. They still behave as though the game were not decided, the battle not fought; we must still reckon with them, but fundamentally we must cease to fear them any more. If you have heard the Easter message, you can no longer run around with a tragic face and lead the humourless existence of a man who has no hope. One thing still holds, and only this one thing is really serious, that Jesus is the Victor.[5]

Did you read in the paper recently that two Japanese soldiers were found in the Philippines, who had not yet heard, or did not believe, that the war had ended fourteen years ago? They continue to hide in some jungle and shoot at everybody who dares approach them. Strange people, aren't they? Well, we are such people when we refuse to perceive and to hold true what the Easter message declares to be the meaning of the Easter story. Sin and death are conquered; God's free gift prevails, his gift of eternal life for us all. Shall we not very humbly pay heed to this message? "Wake up, sleeper, and rise from the dead, that Jesus Christ may be your light!" He, Jesus Christ, who made our history his own and, in a marvelous turn-about, made his wondrous history our own! He in whom the kingdom of the devil is already destroyed! In whom the kingdom of God and of his peace has already come, to us, to you and me, to us all, on the earth and in the whole world![6]

Humankind's most basic anxiety is fear about the future—especially about the ultimate future. But when the Christian message is properly understood, it severs the nerve of this fear. As Barth puts it, the story of mankind is now *his-story*—that is, the story of Christ and the victory he has *already* won over *all* of the powers of darkness. Saint Paul tells us:

For [God] has made known to us in all wisdom and insight the mystery of his will, according to his purpose which he set forth in Christ as a plan for the fulness of time, to unite all things in him, things in heaven and things on earth [Eph. 1:9–10].

Therefore, take courage Lucky Eddie! A "happy ending" is

assured—even for you and your less-than-exemplary sidekick, "Hägar the Horrible"!

HAGAR THE HORRIBLE

A "happy ending" is also assured in the cosmic battle of the *Star Wars* saga. We know, just as sure as all the *Star Wars* shootin', that even though Darth Vader and the Empire may win an occasional *battle,* the outcome of the *War* itself has already been decided. And this, I submit, is also why *humor* is so much a part of the *Star Wars* series. This is not a grim, humorless humanist battle of "man" alone against the universe, as in *2001.* No, there's another "force" at work in the *Star Wars* saga, a force that is infinitely stronger and wiser and kinder than mere folks—folks toughing it out alone in an indifferent cosmos. Therefore it would be highly inappropriate if the *Star Wars* series, to use Barth's words, should "run around with a tragic face and lead the humourless existence" of a story that's not based on hope. For those who love God, Saint Paul tells us, literally "*all* things work together for good" (Rom. 8:28, KJV). It is the belief of those who "are called according to God's purpose," that eventually everyone—even Darth Vader and the Devil—will thankfully serve Christ and worship him:

God has now lifted [Christ] so high, and has given him
the name beyond all names, so that at the name of
Jesus "every knee shall bow," whether in Heaven or
earth or under the earth. And that is why, in the end,
"every tongue shall confess" that Jesus Christ is the
Lord, to the glory of God the Father [Phil. 2:9–11,
J. B. Phillips].

"Even the enemies of God are the servants of God and the servants of his grace," writes Karl Barth.[7] Well, with this kind of triumphant faith in mind, what could be a more appropriate response than laughter?

So there is indeed *faith* embedded in the *Star Wars* saga, and it is a faith strongly marked by triumphal joy and laughter. This is why the series will probably always be more appealing to *younger* people. Older people, like astronomer Carl Sagan, can perhaps be satisfied with a universe that is finally no more than a vast expanse of cold indifference. But younger people, in whom the ability to believe has not yet atrophied, will always need something with far more warmth and love than Sagan's cosmos.

FUNKY WINKERBEAN

I said earlier that "religion" is a do-it-yourself answer to the question of life's meaning, and that one of the ways we can "do" this answer ourselves is to *dream up* these answers ourselves. But there's another important way in which religion can be a "do-it-yourself" answer. And this happens whenever people believe that their response to these answers comes finally from their own "free will."

The New Testament is always very careful in regard to this point. Christian faith, the New Testament tells us, is simply the belief that Jesus Christ alone is "Lord and Savior." And it calls on people to respond to this belief. But at the same time the New Testament realizes that if people believe this response has come finally from themselves and their own "free will," then finally they have remained their *own* lords and saviors. In this case they have ultimately remained, in a very subtle way, "the masters of their own fates and captains of their own souls." And this is *pride* or *self*-confidence or *self*-righteousness. In this way one's *self* is still ultimately trusted, rather than God. And this is why "free will" is so pernicious. It is the loophole through which the *self*-trusting mentality can still keep the upper hand in the lives of many so-called Christians. "Free will" is a virtuous name for a characteristic vice. It is of "religion," not of faith. It is "do-it-yourself" allegiance to God, a *self*-confidence that prevents true allegiance or *God*-confidence.

The New Testament tells us that when we're properly "adjusted" to God, then it is totally by *his* grace—by *his* doing—that we are so adjusted. But of course this is bad news for human pride. Pride would rather "do it itself," pull itself up by its own bootstraps, be in the driver's seat itself. Human pride will always want its right adjustment to be *self*-righteousness. This is why the message that Jesus is *himself* finally the Lord and Savior will always be bad news for pride.

57

But then the question is raised: "If I'm not finally responsible for my obedience to God, then why obey?" That's like saying, "If I'm not finally responsible for this excruciating toothache, then why bother to do anything about it?" The powerful Force who commands us to obey doesn't just command and let it go at that. He also backs up this command with serious here-and-now consequences when we don't obey. This is why true Christian obedience—or faith—leaves no room for pride. We obey not to do God a favor but to do ourselves a favor. Christian obedience—or faith—is never something we initiate ourselves.

HI AND LOIS

So, then, there are two ways we can try to follow God: either humbly or arrogantly. But if we really succeed in following him, it will always be humbly, by his grace, and never arrogantly, by our "free will." And these two attitudes toward God, arrogance and humility, are also two attitudes toward "the Force" that are found in the *Star Wars* series. Han Solo (whose name means "alone," of course), can say of "the Force":

"I've been from one end of this galaxy to the other,"
the pilot boasted, "and I've seen a lot of strange
things. Too many ... to think that there could be some
such controlling one's actions. I determine my
destiny—not some half-mystical energy field" [p. 121,
Star Wars].

But in *The Empire Strikes Back,* Luke asks Yoda how one can distinguish "the good side from the bad side" of "the Force." And Yoda makes clear that our relationship to the Force's good side is at bottom a *passive* relationship:

"You will know," Yoda answered. "When you are at peace . . . calm, passive. A Jedi uses the Force for knowledge. Never for attack" [p. 134].

And later we are told:

Luke had at last begun to detach himself from the emotion of pride. He felt unburdened, and was finally open to experience the flow of the Force [p. 140].

But, at the same time, we know that *finally* "the Force" will be with everyone. With everyone? Yes, because in the first place, Christians are given the job of *praying* that God "the Force" will finally be with everyone:

Such prayer [for all people] is right, and approved by God our Saviour, whose will it is that all men should find salvation and come to know the truth. For there is one God, and also one mediator between God and men, Christ Jesus, himself man, who sacrificed himself to win freedom for all mankind [1 Tim. 2:3–6 NEB].

We were told to pray the prayer, and we were also told by Christ that "whatever you ask in my name, I will do it" (John 14:13). Therefore, "Courage!" . . . to *all* the people. . . .

SMITHEREENS

"... AND MAY THE FORCE BE WITH YOU. AMEN."

11-26

E.T. and "The Ache of Universal Love"—Closer to Christ Than Even the Churches Are?

E.T.—A Retelling of the Gospel Story

"I don't think [E.T.'s] anything like 'The Wizard of Oz.' Maybe they keep saying that because E.T. kept saying 'Home.' I think it's more like 'Peter Pan' in that if you keep hoping and believing, fairies will be real. And then there's the Christ symbolism."[1]

These are the words of Melissa Mathison, the young writer of the *E.T.* screenplay. She ought to know. And indeed there is plenty of *Peter Pan* in *E.T.* Almost as if to re-emphasize George Lucas's strong insistence on a culture's constant need for value-communicating myths, *E.T.* draws many obvious parallels between itself and the *Peter Pan* story. Instead of *Peter Pan*'s dreaded Captain Hook with his menacing iron hook always at his side, the leader of E.T.'s enemies always wears an ominous ring of jingling keys at *his* side. Both *Peter Pan* and *E.T.* revolve around children, the only people still capable of believing in fairy tales and escaping the limited imaginations of the adult world. At one point in *E.T.* we listen in on the actual *Peter Pan* story as the children's mother reads it to Gertie, the youngest of the three children (pp. 131–33).[2] Instead of Peter Pan, the little boy who teaches the story's children to fly, we have E.T., the little "extra-terrestrial" who also introduces children to flying but also wants to "go home" and to remain an extra-terrestrial. And instead of Tinker Bell, the little fairy who saves Peter Pan and the children from Captain Hook, we have the bell-like

61

spaceship that finally rescues from world-bound authorities not only E.T. but also the children's hopes and dreams.

So there *is* a lot of *Peter Pan* in *E.T.*, but in *Peter Pan* there's also lots of Christ. Most stories—just like most *people*—in "Christendom," contain an enormous conscious or unconscious indebtedness to the Christ story, and *Peter Pan* is no exception. James Barrie, the author of *Peter Pan,* was preoccupied from his earliest years, and especially in *Peter Pan,* with the Christian meaning of death and immortality. Tinker Bell's sacrifice of herself to save Peter Pan's life, which is mentioned in *E.T.*, has obvious Christian overtones (p. 132).

"And then there's the Christ symbolism," to return to Melissa Mathison's words. That is, there's the symbolism that comes to us more *directly* from Christ, and isn't rerouted through *Peter Pan.* And if there's a fair amount of *Peter Pan* in *E.T.*, of "Christ symbolism" there's a flood. Both E.T. and Christ are "extra-terrestrials," coming into the world from "outside in." Both begin their "adventures on earth" in less-than-auspicious circumstances—E.T. in a shed behind the home where he takes up residence, Christ in an animal shelter behind the "inn." Both are males and nothing to look at: E.T. is positively scary until you get to know him, and Christ in Isaiah's well-known prophecy

had no form or comeliness that we should look at him, and no beauty that we should desire him. He was despised and rejected by men; a man of sorrows and acquainted with grief; and as one from whom men hide their faces he was despised, and we esteemed him not [Isa. 53:2–3].

Both have miraculous powers of healing and other powers over nature, and both are marked by great compassion. Both are hunted down by the reigning ideological authorities, both die at the hands of these authorities, and both are resurrected from the dead, appearing at first only to their most trusted companions. After E.T. is "raised from the dead," there's even an "empty tomb" scene. While the authorities believe E.T. to be dead, the children know differently and whisk him away in a van. As they help E.T. down from the back of the van, he's covered in a shroudlike white cloth. The police then finally catch up with the van and "when the doors were fully opened, it was seen to be empty" (p. 237).

Before E.T. "ascends" into the heavens in the spaceship that has returned to rescue him, many of his departing words to his companions, the children, are strikingly similar to final words given by Christ to his disciples. "'I'll be right here,' [E.T.] said, fingertip glowing over Elliott's chest" (p. 246). "I am with you always," Christ tells his disciples before his own ascension (Matt. 28:20).

Indeed, the entire relationship between E.T. and Elliott is drawn very much along the lines of the relationship between Christ and his disciples. Elliott is the ten-year-old boy who takes E.T. into his heart and hides him in his bedroom closet, and Elliott knows that he has been *chosen* for this special friendship with E.T., rather than the choice being his own. He knows he *has* to follow E.T. There is a strong echo here of the disciples' answer to Jesus when Jesus asked them if they would leave him: "Lord, to whom shall we go? You have the words of eternal life" (John 6:67–68). At the same time, the special telepathic link between E.T. and Elliott suggests the Holy Spirit, or "Comforter," which came to be the special spiritual link between Christ and his followers. Elliott, the novel tells us,

knew this thing had been handed to him from the stars,
and he had to follow or—or die.
"You'll like it in here," he called through the door
[to E.T.]. His mind and body moved almost without
effort, signals pulsing inside him. He couldn't know
that a cosmic law had touched him, gyrating him in a
new direction; he only knew he felt better than he'd
ever felt before [pp. 64–65].

In *E.T.* the film, there are nice touches that don't appear in *E.T.* the book. For instance, there's the large Enter sign on Elliott's bedroom door. This sign is in perfect keeping with the statement of Christ that "unless you turn round and become like children, you will never enter the kingdom of Heaven" (Matt. 18:3, NEB). This special childlike quality of faith is a theme constantly being played on in *E.T.*, in both film and book.

On the other hand, there are many fascinating parallels between E.T. and Christ that are drawn in William Kotzwinkle's fine novel but not seen in the film. For instance, when E.T. dies, hardly noticed is

the momentary flicker in the lights, and in the
equipment, nor did they fully perceive the trembling of
the house, the valley. This was reserved for other men,

other equipment, those that monitor disturbances deep in the Earth's core [p. 229].

We are likewise told that when Christ died, "the earth shook, and the rocks were split" (Matt. 27:51).

Both E.T. and Christ arrive on earth at night, and hence they arrive during a literal darkness that is symbolic of a more profound spiritual situation. While Christ was born "by night," in him "the people who sat in darkness have seen a great light" (Luke 2:8; Matt. 4:16). Stranded and alone in the darkness of a California night, E.T.'s first contact with humanity is with a little family who is sitting at dinner and is deeply troubled by the fact that the father of this family has left them. Kotzwinkle's description of the distress of the mother (Mary) applies to the family as a whole: "God, she needed a lift so badly . . ." (p. 17).

But then E.T. himself could also use a lift, because he's been unintentionally left on earth by his fellow extra-terrestrials when their spaceship—"a gigantic old Christmas tree ornament" (p. 1)—took off without him. E.T.'s solution to this problem is to "phone home." His "E.T. phone home!" becomes a byword in both film and book, and as this kind of familiar saying, it's not a bad one to remember. For years signs like the one below have been reminding us that prayer as communication with God is a vitally important part of the "community of the saints."

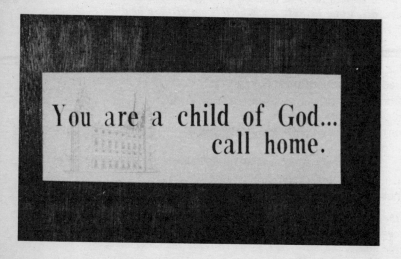

You are a child of God...
call home.

E.T. and Keys to "the Truth"

While it would be possible to continue listing analogy after analogy between E.T. and Christ, it's probably best to stop at this point and let the film's viewers and/or the book's readers do their own homework. Also, as several commentators have pointed out, there are places where this general likeness between the two stories doesn't work out. But this is not surprising. *E.T.* was never intended to be analogous to the Christ story in the first place. And where did I pick up this interesting little bit of information? The Melissa Mathison interview continues in this way:

> *Mathison, educated in a Catholic school in Hollywood, said that during the filming of E.T. she and the cinematographer suddenly realized the similarities between her plot and the story of Jesus Christ: "His being left on Earth, being found, His apostles, dying, the resurrection.*
> *"We were cracking up when we figured out that one. When we told Steven, he said, 'I'm Jewish, and I don't want to hear anything about this.'"*

"Steven," of course, is Steven Spielberg, the creator of *Close Encounters* and the producer-director of *E.T.*

Well, then, are all of these analogies between the Christ and the *E.T.* stories invalidated because they were never intended? Hardly. It goes back to our theory of the "keys." Because we're all trying so hard to find the one correct key for the closed locks of our hearts, either our great need or our unconscious memories—or both—will cause even incorrect keys to resemble the true one. And this is, no doubt, what has happened in *E.T.*—Spielberg's Devil's Tower key has simply grown more and more to resemble the true key.

This is another reason I almost levitated out of my theater seat when I first saw *E.T.* I had been using this illustration of "keys" to talk about "the religion of outer space," and then here come Mathison/Spielberg with their extremely Christ-like extra-terrestrial and their heavy use of *keys* as an obviously pregnant symbol. Was I seeing things or did everything really fit this well?

In *E.T.* the book, the technocrat whose "signature" is the huge collection of jingling keys on his belt and who is in charge of the whole project of capturing a real, live extra-terrestrial, is called—appropriately enough—"Keys." And this is doubly appropriate when we consider that for "Keys" the capture of an outer space alien will unlock the secret of the universe, it will be the Key to the whole meaning of life. To capture E.T. will be to have the Truth nailed down. Truth would then literally be "under lock and key."

But this is not the way "Truth" is come by. "Truth is subjectivity," as Kierkegaard could say. And by that he meant that Truth is never objective knowledge or "objectivity." "Spiritual truths . . . are spiritually discerned," is the way Saint Paul could put it (1 Cor. 2:13–14). And the spirit is not the kind of bird that enjoys being "objectively" nailed down or placed in this kind of cage. The spirit, like the wind, "blows where it wills," said Jesus; "you hear the sound of it, but you do not know where it comes from, or where it is going" (John 3:8, NEB).

This is why we distrust "the Spirit of truth, whom the world cannot receive, because it neither sees him nor knows him" (John 14:17). "No man has power to retain the spirit" (Eccles. 8:8) or to control it or to lock it up in some kind of objective box. For if we did, whatever gave us control or authority over the spirit would logically *itself* be a higher power or authority or god or spirit or "Truth." And how would we then know that *this* God was really the True one? Obviously we are ultimately thrown back on ourselves for deciding what the Truth actually is. Thus "Truth is subjectivity." And this is an uncomfortable position to be in. No wonder we'd rather see Truth "proven" by mystery, miracle, or authority or by any other objective criterion. Like "Keys" we'd rather see "the Truth" snugly secured in a warehouse somewhere.

In the New Testament, "keys" are mentioned by Jesus only once. And that's when the apostle Peter, after the other disciples have tried to hide behind all sorts of *outside* authorities for deciding who Christ is, finally says solely on the basis of his own *belief*—his own *inside,* gut-level, heartfelt, "subjective" belief—"You are the Christ, the son of the living God." Jesus then tells him that in this kind of assurance Peter has "the keys of the Kingdom of heaven." He further says to Peter that "flesh and blood has not revealed this to you, but my Father who is in heaven" (Matt. 16:13–19). So, then, the keys that Jesus spoke of can never be objective knowledge or owned or put on a handy "flesh and blood" ring to wear at one's side. Faith is at least like music in that "objective Truth" is definitely singing "off key."

E.T. and the Quality of God's Mercy

In one of the many newspaper articles that have compared E.T. with Christ, an interesting question was raised. The reporter was asking various people about *E.T.*'s popularity, and in an exchange with Protestant minister William Boyle, he ended his article by letting his own important question out of the bag.

"I think there's a real longing in people's hearts for the spiritual," Boyle said. "There's a natural longing in our hearts for God and our creator, so when you touch on areas of spirituality, I think you see a longing for a meaning outside of ourselves."

If that's true, why aren't people lining up outside churches instead of movie theatres?

Maybe, Boyle said, organized religion hasn't been able to communicate that message to the public.

Not as well as an E.T., anyway.[3]

It may be that what we have in *E.T.* is merely a matter of *better communicating* the same basic message that we get from the churches. But I don't think so. I'm convinced that in *E.T.* a *better God* is being put forward than the one usually dispensed by the churches. What *E.T.* is really pointing to, as I see it, is "the quality of eternity"—or "the quality of God's mercy," to put it another way. And the quality of God's mercy or eternity that we see in *E.T.* is, I believe, an infinitely higher quality than what we find in "traditional" western Christianity.

"Well, it just goes to show you what people want and need," my friend Edith was saying as she stood by the cashbox, selling coffee and sweetrolls in the hospital cafeteria. "And that's love, love, and more love."

And Edith hadn't even seen or read *E.T.* She'd only heard people talking about the film and its phenomenal popularity. But that didn't prevent Edith from putting her finger exactly on *E.T.*'s essence. Not to mention on *people's* essence. Edith and *E.T.* and Charlie Brown all seem to be quite clear on what's *worst* in this world.

PEANUTS

If there ever was a single work of popular art that shows us *precisely* what people—all people—want and need, it has to be *E.T.* That love is *E.T.*'s main attraction and theme there can be no doubt.

Otherwise, for example, the following little scene from *Momma* wouldn't even begin to make sense:

MOMMA

Momma by Mell Lazarus. Courtesy of Mell Lazarus and Field Newspaper Syndicate.

But the love being strongly suggested in *E.T.* is much bigger and better than the love we find in an ordinary human—or even an ordinary Hollywood—"love story." It's also much bigger and better than the love we hear of from an ordinary "Christian" sermon. Hence those long lines outside of *E.T.*'s box offices. Obviously *E.T.* speaks to a deep and widespread unfilled need.

Writing in *Commonweal,* the reviewer of *E.T.* had these interesting observations to make about the creators of science fiction (or "sci-fi") in general, and about one of the creators of *E.T.* in particular:

Their substitute religion is based on an unspiritual premise: something physical is going to save or destroy us, depending on whether the E.T.'s involved are angelic or satanic. If extra-terrestrial intelligence exists, however, it might just be morally mediocre, however bright in engineering. . . . It never occurs to any sci-fi writer . . . that alternate physical worlds, whatever differences of their creatures in size and shape, must in the nature of things be as gray as ours, as haunted by defect and excellence. Such imaginings would demythologize the skies, and bring us back to square one, where real belief in the spiritual was required. Spielberg's limit is that things inhabit the other side of his things. But other worlds aren't other, and salvation is more uncanny than special effects.[4]

In other words, "the gospel from other worlds" can't really be gospel (or good news) because all other *worlds* are finally going to be as finite as our own. *All* creation is subject to exhaustion and death and all the other incompletenesses that come from being merely creation rather than being the Creator. "Other worlds" are not really "Wholly Other," as Karl Barth has referred to God. They are not transcendent, perfect, infinite, or "spiritual," to use our reviewer's word.

O.K. I think this is a good point (especially since it's partially a point I've been trying to make). But now I want to add a couple of "counterpoints" to this reviewer's composition as it pertains to *E.T.* First, there are plenty of indications that *E.T.* does represent the spiritual rather than just the "physical." *E.T.* is more concerned with belief and the supernatural than with super-knowledge and the natural. This is especially evident, for example, in *E.T.*'s use of the *Peter Pan* theme:

["Tinker Bell] says she thinks she could get well again if children believe in fairies! Do you believe in fairies? Say quick if you believe!"

"I do," said Gertie.

"I do," said the ancient space traveler, tears forming in the corners of his eyes [p. 132].

There's a scene in *E.T.* the book where

Elliott looked up at the stars and tried to imagine which one belonged to his new friend.

They all belong to him, said a whisper from the moonlight [p. 94].

All the stars belong to E.T.? What manner of mere extra-terrestrial is here? What sort of "physical" spaceship leaves—as we see in the final seconds of the film—a rainbow in its wake?

But secondly, even if we were to return to "square one"—to the spiritual or to the typical message of the churches—something is dreadfully amiss here. The mere fact that a message speaks of spiritual things doesn't make that message correct or even an improvement on "unspiritual" messages. Indeed, I submit that most so-called spiritual messages are actually *religious* messages, as I've attempted to define "religion." And religion can be absolutely demonic in its results. So while our reviewer faults *E.T.* for not being "spiritual" enough, I'm saying that it is indeed spiritual, and furthermore that its spirit would seem to be much closer to the true spirit of Christ than a lot of what we hear coming from the churches.

If we let E.T. = Eternity, then again, the *quality* of eternity being dramatized in *E.T.* is literally one "hell" of a better eternity than the one usually being described by the churches. And why is this? Because the gospel according to *E.T.* is much more obviously and consistently and completely a gospel of *love*. *E.T.* points to a universal love without even a hint of a literal "hell."

The churches also dispense a "gospel of love," but ordinarily . . . typically . . . by and large . . . commonly . . . generally speaking . . . this "gospel of love" heard from the churches is at bottom a "gospel at gunpoint." That is, this gospel claims to speak of a great love, but only one step behind this "love" is an unspoken or often very vocal great threat—the threat of an eternity in "hell" if we refuse this love. What a travesty of "love"—even *human* love, not to mention God's. For one would think that God's love ought to be *at least* as great as what human beings are capable of.

PEANUTS

But, I contend, it is precisely the implied or expressed threat of eternal perdition that compromises the churches' "gospel of love," that gives this "gospel" the lie to ordinary people, and is in fact behind by far most of the atheism in "Christendom." On the other hand, this is not the quality of mercy we see in *E.T.* In *E.T.* we get the strong feeling of an infinite, unconditional, no-strings-attached love for *all* people. At the same time this love communicated through *E.T.* is all-powerful and sovereign. It is not so flimsy and pitifully weak that it can be finally frustrated or defeated by mere human whim or by meager man's arrogant illusion called "free will."

Kotzwinkle's "novelization" of *E.T.* has, I believe, captured not only the specifics but also the spirit of Melissa Mathison's screenplay. And in the novel there is a moving scene in which Elliott lies in a forest looking up at the stars while he keeps watch over E.T.'s homemade transmitter to the stars. As Elliott "spread his arms in the grass" a soft voice begins to speak to him through the wind:

> *The voice whispered to him, opening his youthful mind, wider, wider.*
>
> *Still bound to their planet, Earthlings cannot deal with the ache of universal love, said the golden whisper echoing through the endless corridors. . . . The message shot through his whole being—a message meant to be carried by a creature much more evolved than himself, a creature whose inner nature was such that it could love a star and be loved in return by the overwhelming solar force.*
>
> *The music of the spheres devoured him, taking his meager little Earth-soul and overwhelming it with the ecstasy of the cosmos, against which Earthlings by birth are shielded [pp. 172–73].*

This is, I believe, a perfect description of the love that speaks to us through *E.T.,* a love eternal, universal, and finally victoriously overwhelming all enemies. It's also a fair description of the message of God's love for all humankind as this message has been "carried" to us by Christ.

But if it really is the threat of eternal damnation that prevents a proper understanding of the goodness of "the good news" of Christ, a threat that prevents the good news from being appreciated as being as loving and good as it actually is, then, first, where does this threat come from and, secondly, why has this threat's staying power proven so strong in the history of the church? Or, to sum up these two questions in terms of *E.T.,* when will we earthlings ever be able to ''deal with the ache of universal love''?

As to the first question, the gospel of God's universal love and ultimate salvation of *all* people is a message that's *hidden* in the New Testament in a kind of hard protective wrapper. In the New Testament, this tough protective outer shell is usually referred to as ''the law.'' And it is ''the law'' that contains the threat of eternal damnation. The message of the gospel of Christ, on the other hand, contains no such threat of hell and even denies the existence of such a final reality.

But then the question naturally arises: Why, then, is the gentleness of the gospel, the really *good* news, clothed in this rough outer garment? Why isn't the unlimited goodness of the Christian message proclaimed more clearly and openly in the New Testament? Why is the bright warm sun of the God who is love sometimes hidden behind this dark, cold cloud of the *law* with its threat of doom and damnation? Why make a secret of such important good news? Won't such hiddenness lead to confusion?

Yes, this kind of hiddenness can and does lead to confusion, and the confusion and trouble caused by the New Testament's original secretiveness has begun to increase unbearably over the years. Nevertheless, this hiding of the gospel's unrestricted goodness was originally a strategy not only serving a good purpose but even made necessary by the historical circumstances in which the church was born. Here is a scene from *Hägar the Horrible* that shows us exactly why the brightness and totality of God's love, revealed in Christ, needed to be hidden at first in something as dark and severe as the law:

HAGAR THE HORRIBLE

As we've already indicated, the law was a *protective* wrapper, a *protective* outer shell in which the gospel was placed. It was a necessary early protection against abuse, similar to the way the infant Jesus was himself hidden for a while to protect him from the cruel dangers of the time. "Do not give dogs what is holy," demanded Jesus, "and do not throw your pearls before swine, lest they trample them under foot and turn to attack you" (Matt. 7:6). Only those whose hearts were sensitive enough and open enough to the message of Jesus would be, he said,

> *granted to know the secrets of the Kingdom of heaven;*
> *but to those others it has not been granted. . . . That is*
> *why I speak to them in parables. . . . There is a*
> *prophecy of Isaiah which is being fulfilled for them:*
> *"You may hear and hear, but you will never*
> *understand; you may look and look, but you will never*
> *see. For this people's mind has become gross; their ears*
> *are dulled, and their eyes are closed. Otherwise, their*
> *eyes might see, their ears hear, and their mind*
> *understand, and then they might turn again, and I*
> *would heal them" [Matt. 13:11, 13–15, NEB].*

To the closedhearted, the parable—and indeed the entire message of Jesus—remains only a parabolic outer shell. Their spiritual dullness makes them incapable of seeing through this message's literal, more superficial meaning. For if Jesus' message of universal love and salvation were more openly announced, it would be open to gross abuse by the "gross at heart." Therefore this message is communicated in a form that remains only a hard law to the hardhearted; but the openhearted will be able to see *through* this law to the gospel.

Goethe once said that "whatever liberates our spirit without giving us self-control is disastrous." And this was a problem of which Jesus and the early church were acutely aware. Saint Paul, for instance, could say of the church's "secret" message: "That secret is Christ himself; in him lie hidden all God's treasures of wisdom and knowledge" (Col. 2:2–3, NEB). And these treasures were to be cautiously protected. Therefore, "Pray that I may make the secret plain," Saint Paul could ask of the churches (Col. 4:4, NEB). For there was always this problem in bringing people beyond the law and into the spiritual maturity of the gospel: "You, my friends, were called to be free men; only do not turn your freedom into license for your lower nature, but be servants to one another in love" (Gal. 5:13, NEB).

The Christian's knowledge and experience of "freedom" in God is, of course, an experience that only comes through obedience to God, through being "servants to one another in love." But the dull of heart will always try to ignore this essential element of obedience in Christian freedom. They will want to hear only the "freedom" part and not the command that comes with it to "be servants to one another in love."

And so the early church, then, promulgated the law alongside the gospel for the same reason that Jesus could say Moses had given the Israelites a law for divorce: *"For your hardness of heart* Moses allowed you to divorce your wives" (Matt. 19:8). But the church's early use of the law was not limited solely to *protecting* the gospel. The law was also used as a means of *penetrating* people's hard hearts and in this way *preparing* those hearts for understanding the gospel. This is why the New Testament can be seen tightening the law and making it even more severe. Jesus, for instance, could say:

"You have learned that our forefathers were told, 'Do not commit murder; anyone who commits murder must be brought to judgement.' But what I tell you is this: Anyone who nurses anger against his brother must be brought to judgement. If he abuses his brother he must answer for it to the court; if he sneers at him he will have to answer for it in the fires of hell" [Matt. 5:21–22, NEB].

In other words, Jesus pushed the law to its inevitable conclusion: before the law we are all guilty and therefore *all* "will have to answer for it in the fires of hell." No wonder the disciples could be driven to ask in desperation: "Who then can be saved?" (Matt. 19:25). Shakespeare has given perfect expression to this New Testament view of "the law" (or divine "justice") when he has Portia say in *The Merchant of Venice:* "In the course of justice none of us/Should see salvation" (IV, i). If it comes to a strict matter of legal perfection then *all* of us are doomed:

BROOM–HILDA

And in this same way the New Testament uses the law's demand for perfection as an *argumentum ad absurdum*—the argument of salvation by obedience to the law is pushed to its absurdly unsatisfying conclusion where *all* people are guilty before God and therefore *all* are doomed to hell. In this kind of everyone-encompassing legal wipeout, people are likely to cry out for mercy, and *mercy* is what the *gospel* is all about. And thus in this way the *bad* news of the law has been used to penetrate hard hearts and prepare them for deep appreciation of the *good* news. That good news is this: mercy for all the guilty, which includes us all. Here, for

example, is how Saint Paul can contrast the all-inclusive guilt under
the law with the all-inclusive mercy of the gospel:

*Then as one man's trespass led to condemnation for all
men, so one man's act of righteousness leads to
acquittal and life for all men [Rom. 5:18].*

*For God has consigned all men to disobedience, that he
may have mercy on all. . . . For from him, and through
him and to him are all things [Rom. 11:32, 36].*

Meanwhile, back to the question about *E.T.*—why aren't people
lining up outside churches as they have at *E.T.*? The answer, I
believe, boils down to this: The divine love we see suggested by *E.T.*
is simple, direct, unambiguous. But the love of God we hear
proclaimed by the churches is all too often muted or timid or
ambiguous or sometimes even corrupted into the direct opposite of
love—namely, fear. And this situation has come about chiefly
because "the law" no longer *protects* the gospel or *prepares* for it
as it did when the New Testament was written. Instead, the law's
threat of damnation has now become the great *preventer* of a
proper understanding and appreciation of the gospel of God's
victorious love. No doubt this hardness surrounding the gospel
originally served the gospel well. But increasingly through the years it
has become a burdensome, useless cargo that prevents the church
from sailing beautifully in the spirit's strong wind—or even floating
very satisfactorily.

But what has brought about this deep change? Why is it true that
the law, as we have defined it, is no longer a help to the gospel of
God's love but has now become a great harm and hindrance to it?
Well, for starters, when the gospel first appeared, the religious law
was about the only law on the books, and therefore there was great
need for the law's "rulebook." But today the civil law exists in
relative independence from any religious law. People are now far
from being solely dependent on the religious commandment to teach
them: "Do not commit murder." The "secular" law now does a good
job of making this clear. *Hägar the Horrible,* with all of his casual
lawlessness, would no longer have it as easy as he once did.

Secondly, Christ emphasizes that a tree can be known by its fruit,
and by this time in the church's history we've had plenty of time to
see and taste the increasingly bitter fruit produced by the law's

threat of hell. Overwhelmingly that fruit has been *atheism.* And this is a matter of historical record. When we examine closely the history of atheism in Western civilization, we can see revulsion from the doctrine of damnation at the root of most of this atheism. Feuerbach was turned away from Christianity by the threat of eternal doom, and from Feuerbach's branch we have the further fruit of people such as Marx, Engels, Lenin, Stalin, and Mao, all of whom also had no love for Christianity because of this teaching. Nietzsche was turned away from Christ by the idea of a loving God punishing his own creatures eternally, and we've already mentioned the fruit of Nazism that grew from Nietzsche's branch. Hitler himself hated "Christianity" for just this reason. It's also clear that Darwin and Freud had no love for Christ because of "his hell."

These names are mentioned simply to point out a few of the main branches or thrusts of modern atheism. They say nothing, of course, about the ordinary man and woman in the pew who have finally decided that they could no longer take such a God seriously. There is a "no more powerful and irrefutable argument in favor of atheism than the eternal torments of hell," wrote Russian theologian Nicolas Berdyaev.[5] "The height which ethical thought has reached may be measured by its attitude toward the idea of eternal hell," he continues. This idea "is one of the chief hindrances to the return of a dechristianized world to Christianity."[6]

So "hell" no longer protects the gospel but only repels people from it. But what about its other earlier function of opening and preparing people's hearts to the true goodness of the gospel? As I hope is now obvious, the harshness of hell now only hardens people's hearts against knowing and loving Christ. But this doesn't mean that the hearts of modern men and women aren't broken and open to receiving some *good* news from *somewhere.* Indeed it is this very here-and-now brokenheartedness that the New Testament is ultimately referring to when it speaks of "hell" and "judgment." When we see through the outward, parabolic form in which the New Testament mentions "hell," we can see that it's talking about the reality of a "judgment" that occurs in the present, in *this* lifetime, *inside* our hearts. For instance, this is why Saint Paul could say, speaking in the present tense: "For we see divine retribution revealed from heaven and falling upon all the godless wickedness of men" (Rom. 1:18, NEB). Some folks worry that if God is finally going to forgive *all* people for their sins and let everyone into heaven, then wickedness will go unpunished. But they don't need to worry about that. Even if the wicked never end up in hell, that doesn't mean that in the meantime hell won't be in them.

BRINGING UP FATHER

"Hell" or "divine retribution" is a suffering—the deepest suffering— that comes from no less than our *present* "terrible hunger" for eternity, or God, in our hearts. So in this sense, hell *is* "eternal" suffering. But it is eternal in its dimension of *depth,* not in its *duration.*

WENDY, LISTEN, "IF THE HISTORY OF THE UNIVERSE COULD BE COMPRESSED INTO ONE YEAR'S TIME, THE EARTH WOULDN'T HAVE FORMED UNTIL MID-SEPTEMBER...

"AND ALL OF MAN'S RECORDED HISTORY WOULD TAKE PLACE IN THE FINAL TEN SECONDS OF THE YEAR."

THAT WOULD MEAN THAT YOU AND I HAVE ONLY KNOWN EACH OTHER FOR JUST THE TINIEST FRACTION OF A SECOND!

IT JUST SEEMS LIKE AN ETERNITY.

FAGAN 10-23

© 1981 United Feature Syndicate, Inc.

DRABBLE

And so modern men and women, having been told that "hell" refers to a future eternal duration caused by legalistic unrighteousness rather than to a present eternal depth caused by the absence of God in our hearts, are in this way left in the only real hell there is. They mistakenly believe that the New Testament has no insight or anything to say about the depth of suffering they now find themselves in—or rather, the depth of suffering they now find in themselves. Instead of appreciating and grasping what the New Testament is really saying about hell, they are turned away from

81

those writings by what they take to be their promise of an even greater suffering to come after death. And in this way the "poor in heart," to whom the gospel's message is directed in particular, continue to go begging and find no genuine *good* news or comfort in the churches. Small wonder that so many people line up for something like *E.T.* In *E.T.,* there's at least the strong suggestion of something resembling truly good news.

Logically, there are only *two* basic ways we can understand Christianity—positively or negatively. Either Christianity finally based on *fear* or Christianity finally based on *love.* Either Christianity as

1. eternal fire insurance, *or as*
2. eternal love assurance.

E.T., we are happy to say, definitely belongs to the second persuasion:

He loved Earth, especially its plant life, but he liked humanity too, and as always when his heart-light glowed, he wanted to teach them, guide them, give to them the stored intelligence of millennia [p. 7].

May E.T.'s tribe increase.

The Long Lines Outside *E.T.* vs. the Long Lines Outside Some Churches

There was a second question we raised back up the road: How can we account for the staying power of the threat of hell in the history of the church? When we examine this threat dispassionately, we can easily see that it has no good theological, ethical, or even biblical argument to stand on. Passion must therefore have something to do with the way it manages to stick around. And so it does.

To put the matter in a nutshell, the threat of hell makes possible a "power trip" that man-unkind passionately loves. The institutional church has especially appreciated the power it could obtain from people's fear of hell. With this kind of power in their hands, the power to damn people or to save them from an eternity of suffering, institutional churches have been able to lead people around by their emotional noses for centuries. Even in this day and age individual clergy can shake down huge salaries and build up enormous followings by trafficking in people's fear of hell. And in addition to wielding this threat, the purveyors of gloom and doom practically have the whole topic of life after death to themselves. Many "liberal" churches scarcely even believe in such a life; and the so-called mainline churches are usually so wishy-washy and ambiguous on the subject, that in them you can believe anything you like—or nothing—about a future life. Most mainline churches would seem to find it preferable to allow the gospel to remain a secret rather than to take a clear stand or to stick one's theological neck out. This is the main reason the mainliners are losing members fast. People like Kudzu can't be expected to follow for long.

KUDZU

What the world needs now is not a "secret" gospel hidden behind a timid ambiguity, or an ultimately *bad* news of hell and the law, but a bold, open, clearly *good* news, a good news much closer to the message we see in *E.T.* And thus the lines forming outside many "conservative" churches—the churches that are not afraid to speak authoritatively about our future, including the danger of hell-fire—can sometimes be as long as the lines outside *E.T.* Indeed, local churches aren't even large enough to contain such a clientele. There are so many folks out there who need *meaning* in their lives, and therefore knowledge about the *future*—whether good news or bad news—that only a "TV ministry" will do:

DOONESBURY

But the law that "power corrupts" also applies to churches or governments or clergy who use this kind of power. They usually end up too greedy or too arrogant or both, and so unwittingly produce either a much-needed reformation or a wholesale defection. In the case of the "wholesale defection," there is a lot of church history beautifully summarized in the following parable from *The Wizard of Id:*

WIZARD OF ID

So institutions are given a very profitable power by people's fear of a literal hell. But then *individuals* are also provided an appealing power by such a belief. If there is a literal hell, obviously it can't be

God's fault if I end up there. I myself must have the power to avoid such a fate. I *myself* will use my own power (or "free will") to be a righteous person and be on God's side, whatever this may involve. Therefore my righteousness is literally *self*-righteousness—and human selfishness loves self-righteousness. Also, if other people have freely used their own power to go it alone without God, I'm certainly justified in seeing myself as a superior person and in looking down on these others, as God himself must see us; and I'm even justified in damning these sinners to hell, as certainly God will. Moreover, because I'm righteously interested in saving other people from spending an eternity in hell, I'm also quite justified in using any and all means to impose my superior will on the sinful and foolish wills of these others. For these others are not only condemning their own souls to eternal perdition, they're also dragging others down with them. Obviously, there is no better way of keeping open the floodgates of human pride and tyranny than keeping open the gates of hell. It works about like this:

DOONESBURY

There is another reason why we tenaciously cling to the fear of hell—namely, the fear of hell itself. When we read the Bible only literally and/or superficially and see that it speaks of "hell," we can easily be spooked by such talk if we don't sense the deeper meaning and reality behind it. And if thus spooked by the Bible, the next thing we will want the Bible to be is a literally infallible, no-nonsense authority that can tell us simply and clearly what we must do to be "saved" from hell. And in this way we become stuck in the trap of biblical literalism, a kind of fearful vicious circle fathered by the fear of hell itself. And thus, "the children of hell" about whom Jesus spoke are still very much with us today:

Woe to you, scribes and Pharisees, hypocrites! for you traverse sea and land to make a single proselyte, and when he becomes a proselyte, you make him twice as much a child of hell as yourselves [Matt. 23:15].

"The children of hell" live under this fear "just to be on the safe side." But in addition to never being absolutely sure of their safety under such an exacting taskmaster, they know it's hell itself *trying* to satisfy all of the law's difficult demands. This was the same hell that Saint Paul was trapped in (and was finally opened up by) before his conversion and as he attempted to live "under the law": "When the commandment came . . . I died; the very commandment which promised life proved to be death to me" (Rom. 7:9–10). And hence one more reason why such children of hell are offended to the core by the idea that finally *all* of God's children will go home to the same Father from whom all came. They don't think it's fair that they live under this harsh, punishing law and others will get off scot-free. It's an old story. Jesus spoke of it in this way:

When it was the turn of the men who had come first, they expected something extra, but were paid the same amount as the others. As they took it, they grumbled at their employer: "Those late-comers have done only one hour's work, yet you have put them on a level with us, who have sweated the whole day long in the blazing sun!" The owner turned to one of them and said, "My friend, I am not being unfair to you. You agreed on the usual wage for the day, did you not? Take your pay and go home. I choose to pay the last man the same as you. Surely I am free to do what I like with my own money. Why be jealous because I am kind?" [Matt. 20:10–15, NEB].

In other words, to those who live outside the gospel and only trust in the severe version of God's "justice" or law, the good news of God's kindness and mercy will sound like bad news every time:

LOLLY

All of this is crucially important to us all, not only *inwardly* but also *outwardly.* And this is because our "quality of life" is do deeply and widely determined by the "quality of eternity" we believe in. The apple never falls that far from the tree. Just as children tend to resemble and imitate their worldly parents, so we all likewise tend to resemble and imitate our "heavenly Father." If that father is loving and kind, we will have strong reasons and support for being the same. If he is harsh and vindictive, we will be justified in emulating this type of father. If we believe we have no father, this will tend to make us bitter and resentful and proud of our ability to make it on our own without a father. Also, without a "Father who art in heaven" our fellow men and women are not our brothers and sisters, but— like us—they are only highly developed animals, and they are easily expendable if they can help us obtain—or if they get in the way of—our here-and-now desires, the only desires left to us if there is no eternity. Nothing has more influence on how people *live now* than what they *believe* about their *future*—especially their ultimate future.

And so Jesus revealed the Gospel of our Father's ultimate mercy, in order, as he said, "that men may have *life,* and may have it in all its fullness" (John 10:10, NEB). Christians are enabled to love because of the assurance—which they have found in following Christ—of God's love. Christians can love because, as Saint John puts it, "[God] first loved us" (1 John 4:19). For each one of us is like Ira. This is why Christ "came down from heaven"—to show us God's "perfect love [which] casts out fear" (1 John 4:18).

At the very close of *E.T.,* the little extra-terrestrial is saying good-bye to his friends, the children, before he boards his spaceship and escapes the fast-approaching danger of "Keys" and returns once more into the heavens. Here are the highlights of that final touching scene as Kotzwinkle's book describes it:

He lifted [Gertie] into his arms. "Be good."
A shadow moved at the edge of the clearing, and the
sound of jingling keys filled the night. E.T. quickly set
Gertie down. . . .
The old voyager embraced the boy, and felt the
cosmic loneliness run through him, as deep as any he'd
ever felt. He touched Elliott's heart, and made the

intricate wave-sign over it with his fingertips. . . .
"I'll be right here," he said, fingertip glowing over
Elliott's chest.
   Then the old botanist walked up the gangplank. The
inner light of the Great Gem glowed above him, and he
felt the millionfold circuits of its awareness lighting
in him, until his heart, like Elliott's, had filled, not
with loneliness but with love [p. 246].

E.T. speaks to us because it's an *embrace* like his that all of us
want and need. What the world needs now is not cosmic fire
insurance, but cosmic love assurance. And people are *desperate* to
find this assurance. This is why the following cartoon makes a kind
of tragicomic sense:

In E.T.'s love we see a love very much like the love that can be
seen in Christ—especially in the *crucified* Christ. For those arms of

91

Christ stretched open on the cross represent the widest possible embrace—an embrace showing us the *extent* of God's love, an embrace encompassing the *entire world.* "God was in Christ," says Saint Paul, "reconciling *the world* to himself, no longer holding men's misdeeds against them" (2 Cor. 5:19, NEB). At the same time, it is in the blood flowing from those impaled hands of Christ that we can see the *depth* of God's love: "Through [Christ] God chose to reconcile the whole universe to himself, making peace through the shedding of his blood upon the cross—to reconcile all things, whether on earth or in heaven, through him alone," Saint Paul tells us (Col. 1:20, NEB). The love of this one person in particular wouldn't be of such decisive, unique significance were it not for *who* this person was: "For in [Christ] the complete being of God, by God's own choice, came to dwell" (Col. 1:19, NEB).

But why "through him alone"? There are a lot of explanations we could advance that make good sense of this "him alone," but ultimately this way through which we all must go is "by God's own choice," as Paul reminds us. From the very earliest traditions of the Bible we learn that "the LORD our God, the LORD is one" (Deut. 6:4). And when the Lord our God decided to come down from heaven and walk among us men and women, he *remained one.* This is why we call Jesus *the* Christ. From the Christ-ian perspective Christ alone is the one from whom we can find the firm eternal love assurance all of us are seeking—an eternal love that ultimately all of us *will* find. Therefore this faith is called "Christian." In the meantime, *E.T.,* by pointing so beautifully to Christ in so many ways, can help us find this assurance now. This is why E.T.'s adventure on earth is so marvelously summed up by the psalmist, and even in the correct order:

Call upon me in the day of trouble [says the Lord];
I will deliver you,
and you will glorify me [Ps. 50:15].

When Elliott's friend Lance finally meets E.T., he says to him softly, "I've . . . dreamt . . . about you . . . all my life" (p. 164). And Elliott tells E.T. when the little space alien dies, "You were like a wish come true. But it wasn't a wish I knew I had, till you came to me" (p. 231). E.T. makes no pretensions of being the wish-fulfiller we all need or another savior or a kind of co-Christ. But he is "like" Christ, the wish come true. He is a very close copy of the original. And that's why we instinctively love him. It's the *quality* of his love that draws us to him.

How excellent is thy loving-kindness, O God!
Therefore the children of men put their trust under the
shadow of thy wings [Ps. 36:7, KJV].

Notes

Chapter 1

1. *Time,* Oct. 7, 1974, p. 11.
2. Quoted in Heinz Zahrnt, *The Question of God,* trans. R. A. Wilson (New York: Harcourt, Brace & World, 1969), p. 44.
3. This relationship, and its origin, between atheism, nihilism, and religion, has been discussed in far greater detail in my book *Something to Believe In.*
4. *The History of Religions: Essays on the Problem of Understanding,* ed. J. M. Kitagawa (Chicago: The University of Chicago Press, 1967), p. 25.
5. *Newsweek,* Jan. 1, 1979, p. 50.

Chapter 2

1. From "The Playboy Interview," in *The Making of Kubrick's 2001,* ed. Jerome Agel (New York: New American Library, 1970), pp. 352–53.
2. Henry Finck, *Richard Strauss: The Man and His Work* (Boston: Little, Brown & Co., 1917), p. 181.

Chapter 3

1. Quoted in Antonina Vallentin, *The Drama of Albert Einstein,* trans. Maura Budberg (Garden City, N.Y.: Doubleday, 1954), pp. 290–91.
2. Dietrich Bonhoeffer, *Letters and Papers from Prison,* ed. Eberhard Bethge (New York: Macmillan, 1971), p. 380.
3. Quotations are from Steven Spielberg, *Close Encounters of the Third Kind* (New York: Dell, 1977).
4. See, for instance, "The Aliens Are Coming," in *Time,* Nov. 7, 1977.
5. *C. G. Jung: Letters,* ed. Gerhard Adler (Princeton: Princeton University Press, 1975), p. 403.
6. C. G. Jung, *Flying Saucers: A Modern Myth of Things Seen in the Skies,* trans. R. F. C. Hull (Princeton: Princeton University Press, 1978), pp. 35–36.
7. Jor-El's speeches are quoted from "Chauvinist Messiah," Ed Spivey, Jr., *Sojourners,* March 1979.

8. *Superman—The Movie—Magazine* (New York: D.C. Comics, 1978), p. 14.

9. Carl Sagan, *Broca's Brain* (New York: Ballantine Books, 1980), p. 67.

Chapter 4

1. The "Star Wars" books quoted are George Lucas, *Star Wars* (New York: Ballantine Books, 1976), and Donald F. Glut, *The Empire Strikes Back,* based on a story by George Lucas (New York: Ballantine Books, 1980).

2. "George Lucas Believes in the Force of Myths, Fairy Tales," interview with Joanne Waterman Williams, *Chicago Sun-Times,* May 18, 1980.

3. Bruno Bettelheim, *The Uses of Enchantment* (New York: Vintage Books, 1976), pp. 7–8, 11–13.

4. Lucas interview, *Chicago Sun-Times.*

5. Karl Barth, *Dogmatics in Outline,* trans. C. T. Thomson (New York: Philosophical Library, 1949), pp. 122–23.

6. Karl Barth, *Deliverance to the Captives,* trans. Marguerite Wieser (New York: Harper & Brothers, 1961), pp. 149–50.

7. Karl Barth, *Church Dogmatics,* Vol. II/2, Authorized Trans. (Edinburgh: T. & T. Clark, 1957), p. 92.

Chapter 5

1. Andrew Epstein, "The woman behind the boom: Melissa Mathison pens the bonanza called 'E.T.,'" *Chicago Tribune,* August 15, 1982, copyright © by Los Angeles Times Syndicate.

2. Page numbers refer to William Kotzwinkle, *E.T.: The Extra-Terrestrial in His Adventure on Earth* (Universal City, Calif.: MCA Publishing, 1982).

3. Tom Webb, "Religion Goes to the Movies," *Chicago Tribune,* Aug. 17, 1982, copyright Knight-Ridder Newspapers.

4. Tom O'Brien, "Very High Sci-Fi," *Commonweal,* Aug. 13, 1982, pp. 442–43.

5. Nicholas Berdyaer, *Dream and Reality,* trans. Katherine Lampert (New York: Macmillan Co., 1951), p. 293.

6. Ibid., p. 131.

85939